Divine Humanness

DIVINE

HUMANNESS

by

AARNE SIIRALA

Translated by T. A. KANTONEN

FORTRESS
PRESS

PHILADELPHIA

To My Wife Kaisa

233
Si2d
9/935
Jan. 1975

Translated from the Finnish
Jumalallinen inhimillisyys by Aarne Siirala
Werner Söderström, Helsinki, 1968

© 1970 by FORTRESS PRESS

Library of Congress Catalog Card Number 70–99460

2312G69   Printed in U.S.A.   1-299

Contents

Preface

This study was written in 1967, the year which marked the fiftieth anniversary of Finland's independence, the hundredth of the Canadian Federation, and the four hundred and fiftieth of the Reformation. The dynamics of all these traditions reverberate in this study.

I owe a debt of gratitude to the supportive community of learning at Waterloo Lutheran University, and to a large web of friends on both sides of the Atlantic Ocean. Among these, Jean and Sidney Lanier and Edwin S. Webster, Jr., gave a quite unique inspiration, which they moreover went on to make tangible in the form of financial support.

To Professor Taito A. Kantonen I want to express my enduring appreciation for his translation.

Chapter One

Man the Explorer

It has been said that science is fundamentally a matter of making right guesses.[1] The scientist is impelled by an apprehension of unknown reality, coupled with the awareness that his very definition of his problem, the formulation which is to give direction to his research, may become an obstacle to establishing contact with that reality. Scientific work is exploration. On the ship of research the compass needle and the chart are constantly being consulted, but the exploration itself is carried forward by an urge toward the unknown.

This urge has deep roots in human existence. The development of a child takes place in an exploratory manner. A growing contact with the unknown generates in the mind ever broader assumptions and surmises, and their viability is weighed in the scales of experience. A child's growth is disturbed if for some reason or other he is unable to live as an explorer. The first contact with the unknown may be such as to cause the traveler to direct his ship back to the shore, because neither the motivation of those who launched his ship nor the whole cruise appears to make sense. The contours of what lies ahead may also turn out so often to be illusions and mirages that the voyager is left to flounder about in the same waters and to concentrate only on the preliminary tasks, checking compass and chart. Fear of the unknown may indeed make him slave to his chart in such measure that the ship drifts past undiscovered worlds. Whatever the reasons may be, abandoning the exploration proves fatal, especially at certain stages of human growth.

Imbedded in human nature are also other potentialities for growth which may be considered as more important than the development of the exploratory drive. The scientist shows by his choice of vocation that he regards exploration to be life's central

direction of growth. This is a personal decision which he has
to make. It is impossible to prove to a man in retreat from
exploration, a man severely hurt and disappointed by his skir-
mishes with life, that there are unknown realities which he should
explore. It is just as impossible to prove that one direction of
human growth is necessarily more important than others. Scientific research is based on the conviction that the widening
contact with reality obtained and mediated through knowledge
has basic importance for life. The methods and goals of scientific
research are understood differently in various disciplines, but
common to all work done in the name of science is trust in the
possibility of building by means of creative hypotheses, guesses,
and questions a bridge from the knowledge already obtained to
the reality which has remained unknown. Furthermore, it is the
conviction of science that this bridging and the discovery of new
knowledge thus afforded is possible on the basis of hypotheses
drawn from the world of experience and verifiable within it (the
principle of verification). Scientific research is impelled by the
passionate effort to discover ever deeper and broader and more
productive contacts with reality, and it is guided by the conviction that the contacts which it seeks are found and sustained solely
by respecting human experience as the only scales in which hypotheses and theories are to be weighed. This approach does not
necessarily negate the validity of other approaches to reality. It
leads, however, to a firm adherence to the point of view that where
the basic thrust of science is not respected, there one excludes
oneself from the community of science and its universe of discourse.

Human Quest—Divine Truth

By now the reader is probably ready to ask: What does a
study bearing the title *Divine Humanness* have to do with scientific research? Does not theology by its very use of such a
concept as "God" exclude itself from scientific discourse? Is not
theological discussion about a divine revelation which illumines
the depths of reality in irreconcilable contradiction with the

questing spirit of scientific study? Does not theology regard divine truth as so absolute and certain and human experience as so relative and uncertain that the use of experience as standard and criterion must be denied?[2] In short, are not the divine and the human mutually exclusive?

We shall examine these questions together with the reader, convinced that they are unavoidable in the search for a contact with reality which affords valid new knowledge. The starting point is the hypothesis that to experience reality as an encounter between the divine and the human, and hence to speak of God and the divine as manifest in the encounter, is an essential element of the empirical world which is the object of scientific research. The present study participates in the scientific discussion which is taking place concerning the nature of human experience. It shares the basic presuppositions of the explorers. The encounter between the divine and the human, what happens in that encounter and how it is expressed, will be studied from the point of view of scientific exploration. The results of this intended study are to be weighed in the scale of scientific discussion in the same way as experiences derived from reality in other ways and expressed differently.

Theological participation in discussion based on empirical research may be attacked both from the side of science and from the side of faith. Reference has already been made to the fact that when science is true to its own basic presuppositions it cannot admit into its community of discussion those who question its whole effort to remain open to reality and to new knowledge and who deny in principle the use of human experience as the criterion for the validity of knowledge. The authenticity of adherence to the letter and spirit of the scientific approach will of course become evident only after the participant has made his contribution. The adoption of such an approach indicates in any case the kind of discussion for which the contribution is intended and in which it is to be heard and evaluated. The question to be investigated in the present study is this: In the search for an understanding of the structure and nature of human experience, what is the significance of the kind of experience which leads a man to speak of encounter with divine realities and to seek contact with them?

Theology and Human Experience of the Divine

Western Christian theology in the main has regarded itself as the interpreter of a divine revelation given in Christianity. The nature of this task has been defined in many ways in the various stages of the history of Christendom.

The primary task of theology has often been conceived as the definition of the nature of the church which functions as the mediator and custodian of divine revelation.[3] Theology thus becomes a discussion within the church concerning its own identity and nature. Theology creates the criteria for judging whether the activity and teaching of the churches are in harmony or in discord with divine revelation.

Alongside this church-centered theology of revelation with its many variations, a second major type of revelation theology may be distinguished, namely, nature-centered theology. From this point of view the divine revelation manifest specifically in Christianity, its sacred writings, its history, and its churches, confronts man already in nature and in all experience. The central task of theology thus becomes the creation of a synthesis between general and special revelation. Theology must show how the two kinds of revelation are connected, how special revelation is founded on the experience obtained from the realm of nature.

A third conception of the task of theology is the extremist view that theology is nothing less than a direct continuation of revelation or at least its fundamental vehicle. Thus the most important object of theological study is theology itself, its history and its ongoing discussion. The clarity or eclipse of divine revelation is so decisively dependent on theology that the analysis of its nature and content is confined to a discussion among theologians.

These three streams of thought give rise to three basic types of approach to scientific thinking.

The church-centered view, according to which only the divine revelation given in Christianity affords the knowledge and the experience for understanding man and his world, leads ultimately to the effort to make science serve the church. A theology which seeks to show how science can be a tool in the service of a revelation mediated by Christianity runs into inevitable conflict with the exploring spirit of science. In the phases and structures of Christianity where this view has become dominant, the scientific spirit and the empirical study engendered by it have met severe opposition. Within the structure of the church-centered approach belong also the views which restrict theology to problems entirely outside the field of scientific research. The divine revelation continued in the Christian message is thus understood as confronting man with totally new problems which concern his deliverance from bondage to the world studied by science. Theology is thus given the task of showing that Christianity and science have in fact nothing to do with each other. The only concern of theology is to serve the activity and the proclamation which aims at the realization of a divine plan of salvation. It is only if science intrudes upon questions of man's salvation, which are none of its business, that theology has reason to deal with problems of the relation between Christianity and science.

On the other hand, if the inner logic of a nature-centered theology of revelation is consistently followed, the resulting emphasis is that the scientific enterprise is not only born out of Christian influence but is also the most authentic expression of the Christian spirit. Divine revelation has called and directed mankind to scientific exploration. Thus the task of theology is to ally itself with science in clearing the way for a questing experiential approach to life. The end result of this view is to bring about the same kind of conflict between theology and church as church-centered theology causes in the relations between theology and science. The one seeks to subordinate science into the service of the divine spirit operating in the life of the church. The other aims at cleansing the life of the church from the prescientific elements which obstruct the surge of the spirit of Christian revelation in the search for scientific truth.

From the theology-centered point of view the task of science is defined solely on the premises of theology itself. Theological study is confined within its own closed circle. Theology as the interpreter of divine revelation seeks to determine the functions of science in a divine plan of salvation. Theology thus has the character of pure monologue. Dialogue with the sciences is neither necessary nor possible.

As different as these three conceptions of the task of theology are, in one respect they manifest the same fundamental orientation. In some way or other they all regard as the self-evident starting point and presupposition of theology the avowal or at least assumption that Christianity contains a divine revelation which transcends all other human experience or in any case unveils its true nature. There may be disagreement as to how the essence of Christianity and of the revelation contained in it is to be interpreted, but all are agreed that the fundamental nature of theology is the interpretation of revelation. Since the present study does not proceed from this basic assumption but posits its discussion on entirely different grounds, it is appropriate to answer, if only in a preliminary way, a question unavoidably raised in the mind of the reader: Are we here dealing with theology at all?

The whole following presentation is in fact an attempt to answer this question. Here a few observations may be made which will enable the reader to grasp what is to be said in the context in which it is intended to be understood. The purpose may be achieved by stating at the outset what this study is not about. The aim of what has been said thus far has been to indicate that this study is not a contribution to a discussion in which Christians, churches, and theologians seek to make clear to themselves and to one another the "essence of Christianity" and the content of its "divine revelation." The issue is not whether the arguments of the study and their premises are "Christian," "scriptural," or in agreement or disagreement with "divine revelation." The purpose is not to express the "Christian understanding," the "biblical view," or the "revealed truth" on the relation between the divine and the human.

The Limits of Theological Research[4]

Just as the genuineness of our adherence to the principles of scientific discussion can be judged only by what is said and how it is said, such is also the case with our rejection of the traditional types of theological approach. Only from what is presented in the following and from how it is presented does it become clear whether a presentation which follows other than the traditional lines can retain its character as theology.

From the point of view of the theological heritage sketched above, the proposed new departure appears impossible. The only alternative seems to be to show that the premises of traditional theology are untenable and to create in its place a theology with an entirely new set of propositions. The history of theology contains numerous examples of such attempts. At times the effort has been made to supplant the theology of revelation with a natural theology which derives the content of revelation from nature. At other times a God-centered theology has been replaced with a man-centered theology which aims to demonstrate that speech about God and things divine is in fact man's symbolic speech about himself and his own experience. Thus theology is actually anthropology. These and other similar attempts have sought to create in the place of a theology of revelation a theology which does not differ from it in basic structure. The content of revelation is simply drawn from another area of life.

The present study does not seek to supplant the old theology with a new one; nor does it acknowledge that this is the only alternative. Our disengagement from the theology of revelation must therefore have some other basis than questioning the validity of its premises. This is all the more necessary since the material to be presented is taken from the realm of the traditional theology.

The ultimate reason for the stance here assumed is the hypothesis, thus far unproved and bearing the nature of a guess, that the human experience which leads man to speak of encounter with the divine is essentially such that theological research can shed light on it only from a very limited perspective. This is not to deny that the theology of revelation may contain elements which disclose something essential about the nature of this experience. The theology of revelation constitutes an important area in the realm of Christian faith, which is the object of study in Christian theology. It is misleading, however, to regard the theology of revelation as such to be the interpreter of Christian faith. Although it claims to play the role of servant and interpreter of Christian faith and divine revelation, it has actually often had only a tenuous and even nonexistent connection with the faith which it claims to represent. Often it has used divine revelation as a weapon in fighting for causes quite alien to the Christian faith. One can demonstrate that the theology of revelation has at times severed its connection with the revelation it holds to be divine and become the ideology of an ecclesiastical power group, enabling that group to rationalize its policies. Thus one must reject sharply the attempt of the theology-centered approach to use the concepts of the theology of revelation as the main source material for a study of human experience of the divine. Data drawn from this source has limited significance for such a study.

In the following presentation some material from the theology of revelation will be used as a starting point, with the understanding that this conceptual material gives insight into human experience of the divine only from a very limited point of view. Only a small part of this kind of experience can be verbalized. Most of it is outside the sphere of conceptualization. In his efforts to discern the divine within reality man is led above all to deal with acts, to distinguish in them between love and lovelessness, faith and unfaith, the therapeutic and the destructive. Theological study which concentrates solely on an analysis of theological concepts touches only a thin surface layer of human experience of the divine.

Conceptual analysis thus plays a secondary role in a theological study of what it means to be overpowered by the divine. The failure to see the limitations of this role has had serious consequences in the development of theology. When the theology-centered approach in its extreme forms identifies theology with divine revelation, it may be said to show symptoms of theological megalomania. Here the tendency to overestimate the importance of conceptual and verbal expression, which is psychologically quite understandable, no longer remains a mere temptation. The theologian's own position is all the stronger if his conceptual formulation furnishes the basic content of the experience which he studies. If the encounter with the divine is best expressed in thoughts, then the theology which shapes this thinking into precise concepts is the most reliable expression of the content of divine revelation.

Insofar as the following presentation analyzes concepts it is thus compelled deliberately to exclude areas which are highly important for the total task of theology. One of our aims is to show that the analysis of religious language is a one-sided approach which must be supplemented by a broader study of religious experience, representing other starting points and other data.

With these reservations, the main section of our study belongs in the category of conceptual analysis. It deals with a specific theological conversation on the nature of man's experience of God which took place in the context of traditions characterized above as church-centered and revelation-centered. The purpose of the analysis is to show that this theological heritage has something important to say to the study of human experience impelled by the spirit of exploration. Although it refrains from discussing many of the problems of traditional theology, it seeks nevertheless to contribute something to this theology. It does not sever its connection with the theology of the past in the way in which many current philosophical trends dissociate themselves from the classical tradition of philosophy. On the other hand, the analysis of the conversation to be studied will aim to show that church-centered and revelation-centered theology tend to overlook many essential elements in the human experience of God.

The final section will sketch these elements and seek to point out what kind of research an analysis of theological concepts must take into account in order to avoid the megalomania of pretending to be the only interpreter of religious experience, and to play its proper role in the total task of theology.

Research as Open Discussion

In confronting our view with the theology of revelation and in participating in an empirical exploration of the nature of human experience, we are proceeding on the unproved hypothesis that human experience of the divine, when viewed solely in the light of revelation theology, is set in a context which obscures its meaning for human experience as a whole. All assumptions of research in their preliminary phase are only visions and surmises of unknown origin until it has become clear whether they deal with mirages or with genuine discoveries. It is from this point of view that the basic orientation of the present study must be seen. The validity of the hypothesis must be tested in open discussion.[5]

The ultimate motivation for research lies in the depths of the explorer's own being. Some experiences have led him to point his exploration in a specific direction. In this perspective he seeks to make clear to himself whether the direction he has chosen is the right one. Characteristic of the inner rhythm of research is movement in the direction indicated by visions arising from one's own experience and continual return to an examination of these visions in the light of further experience judged to be significant for the research. Thus the inquirer must always study his own being and clarify for himself his own basic convictions. In all research there is an inevitable confrontation with the person of the one doing the research. Sooner or later, at some stage or other, there must be an accounting of the ultimate motives which have instigated the exploration.

Investigation at this depth unveils such a complex network of causes that the explorer is tempted to set aside such questions. He is indeed in danger of becoming so entangled in that network that the research itself is impeded. In many areas of research, therefore, analysis of the basic issues has been avoided for fear of diverting time and energy from experimental study, perhaps even of enervating it. Yet obviously the rhythm of research is broken by the avoidance of the underlying issues. Both the person of the explorer and the vitality of his exploration suffer damage if the tension between the vision-inspired search and the experiential verification disappears. If the investigator refuses to clarify for himself the vitally important thoughts which have inspired and sustained his investigation, he gradually suppresses within himself the passion which gives purpose to his entire study. Creative visions and hypotheses are stifled, and the investigator gradually becomes only a repeater of the thoughts of others, a puppet on the string of a certain set of empirical data.

The harm is not limited to the person of the investigator. When questions of scientific conscience are set aside, the foundations of scientific research and discussion are undermined. The history of science affords countless examples of the use of the principle of verification, the vitally important principle of weighing hypotheses in the scales of experience, not only to prevent the emergence of new creative theories but also to harness science into the service of alien interests. In extreme cases some political or ecclesiastical power group has thus come to determine the boundaries and the goals of science. These examples show that the very existence of science is threatened when scientific research accepts some set of data as the ultimate basis of evaluation, when some area of experience is proclaimed to be the most real, or when some method of analyzing experiments and experience is accepted as the only true method. In a word, there is an irreconcilable conflict between the spirit of science and the spirit which seeks to subject men to serve one single purpose and which absolutizes one type of experience.

The history of science bears evidence of the serious effects, both upon the person of the scientist and upon the progress of scientific work, which have resulted from the invasion of the world of science by theories and hypotheses later proved to be groundless and misleading. The damage has been especially great when such theories have been defended and propagated in the name of science. Many a chapter in the history of science speaks also of the misuse of scientific freedom. Under the banner of the autonomy and freedom of science battles have often been fought for causes foreign to the spirit of science. Under this banner it has also been possible to avoid questions of scientific conscience by striving only for the preservation of a status quo in which science could be carried on without scientific responsibility. Nor has it been rare to unfurl the banner of scientific freedom only on some sectors of the battlefront while submitting meekly to a social system simply because it does not interfere with the arbitrary freedom.

Although one must beware of underestimating the damage done by utopian theorizing and the misuse of scientific freedom, it is most important to remain alert to the dangers inherent in the attempts to quench the exploring spirit of science. When some area or method is absolutized, that is, declared to be the only area or method which transmits reliable knowledge of reality, not only is the freedom of the scientist and his research suppressed but also the roots are cut by means of which research draws strength from the ground in which it grows. Doubt is cast upon the worth and significance of the underlying human experience which has motivated and encouraged the venture of scientific exploration. The result is not only that the person of the explorer is injured and his research is disrupted, but also that the right of a man to grow out of his own background into a unique person is called into question. To suppress the life of scientific conscience has above all the tragic consequence that man endangers thus his growth into a man of conscience.

Just as we have refused to subscribe to a theology which claims to represent the divine revelation, so we shall also seek to combat the approach which demands in the name of science the right to represent the whole of human experience. If it is easy to find in a theology-centered "positivism of revelation" instances of casting doubt on ideas and experiences which contradict it, it is just as easy to set forth examples of a "positivism of science" which in the name of science practices an inquisition of heretics and suppresses creative thinking. Nor is it difficult to demonstrate that in scientific discussion there is talk of a "scientific" world view—an interpretation of reality, a view of life, or a concept of man—in the same way in which theology has claimed universal validity for some ideas by labeling them as "biblical," "conforming to revelation," or "word of God."

A basic temptation inherent in all research is the tendency to identify the part with the whole, to regard as most real the area of reality which is under research. This temptation is inescapable in all research done in the spirit of exploration. This becomes particularly clear in that stage of research in which the investigator has discovered something that compels him to demolish or to reappraise a currently prevalent theory. A new way of observing some detail may alter the whole in such a way as to bring about irreconcilable contradiction between the representatives of the old theory and the exponent of the new. The old and the new thus become mutually exclusive.

The exponent of the new insight or hypothesis must eventually be able to prove that his theory concerns not only isolated details but the whole. In such a case the investigator must stand or fall with his theory. He must prove the breadth of its validity or be forced to abandon it. Only the scientist who is willing to risk his whole being as a scientist, to whom the abandonment of fundamental insights means a denial of the meaningfulness of the whole enterprise of the exploration, can carry research forward. Thus to the very nature of scientific research belongs passionate rejection of misleading opinions and defense of insights held to be true. In specific instances this leads to an inevitable and irreconcilable conflict between scientists. Under these conditions both the defender of the prevalent theory and the exponent of the new one are tempted to absolutize their respective views. The only way out of the impasse of absolutizing is a continuing open discussion inspired by the spirit of exploration.

The following is meant to be a contribution to this open discussion. It does not offer a "theological" answer to questions left open by other sciences, nor does it seek a "scientific" answer to its own questions. This study concentrates above all upon raising questions which will keep open the discussion of its theme.

A Theological Contribution to an Empirical Discussion

In a study marked by the spirit of exploration, especially as it deals with problems of scientific conscience, answers are sought to questions of decisive importance for the shaping and growth of human life. In such research a man seeks to clarify for himself the purpose of life, to discover the boundary between the human and the nonhuman. As stated above, this presentation rests on the assumption that a discovery of this nature is organically related to religious as well as other efforts to discern what is divine in a man's experience and in the world of reality.[6]

We shall first analyze a theological dialogue which took place in the center of the Christian heritage. From the point of view of the task involved, the data could just as well have been selected from the sphere of some other religion or from some thought structure with a theological approach to existence, such as the philosophy of Plato. The selection of this specific body of data, the dialogue between Luther and Erasmus at a crucial stage of the Reformation, as the starting point is due solely to the fact that it raises questions of peculiar importance to the subject under consideration. It provides as object of study "a phase of an eternal quest" in which the traditional solutions both in understanding the encounter with the divine and in examining the world of experience are questioned. In this dialogue ideas which had smoldered for centuries in the ground of both theological and humanistic studies burst into open flame. The fire revealed the artificial nature of many traditional syntheses in the definition of the mutual relationship of the human and the divine as well as of knowledge and experience. It also makes clear that the effort to be faithful to what has been actually experienced as divine and the effort to seek the boundary between the human and the nonhuman are organically bound to each other. The dialogue is a clarification of the nature of divine humanness.

Chapter Two

A Phase of an Eternal Quest

Hardly any discussion in the tradition of western Christendom has been interpreted in so many and in such contradictory ways as the debate between Luther and Erasmus on the relation between divine command and human will, conducted in the middle of the third decade of the sixteenth century.

Perhaps the most widespread interpretation of the nature of this discussion is the one appearing in many general presentations of the history of Western philosophy.[1] Erasmus is usually portrayed as bearer of the banner of humanism and reason, herald of a new age and pioneer of a democratic and scientific spirit, while Luther is characterized as defender of the faith against human thought and intellect.[2] According to this interpretation, Erasmus strives for a synthesis of antiquity and Christianity, human thinking and divine faith, man's endeavors and God's will. Luther, on the other hand, is seen as a dogmatic theologian who tries to show that such bridge-building is impossible. Bertrand Russell,[3] for example, describes Erasmus as a man who has deep contempt for Scholasticism, a man to whom true religion is a matter of the heart, not of the head or of theological hairsplitting. Concerning Luther, Russell says that as a thinker he belongs to the Middle Ages. In his controversy with Erasmus, Luther follows Augustine slavishly, even exaggerates him. The wide acceptance of the view that Erasmus is the champion of reason and Luther fundamentally an irrationalist is indicated by the fact that Luther is seldom mentioned in the general presentations of Western philosophy and history of thought. Most of these include in the parade of Western philosophers and thinkers such theologians as Augustine, Thomas Aquinas, Calvin, and

perhaps Melanchthon, but Luther is not mentioned among those
who have contributed to the development of Western thinking. Nor has it been uncommon for theologians to give the
same interpretation to the debate. Erasmus is said to represent
the classical, traditional synthesis between divine revelation and
human reason, while Luther with his irrational and purely subjective arguments in this debate takes his stand outside traditional
Christian thinking.

Roman Catholic research[4] in particular has criticized the subjectivism of Luther's position, objecting to his procedure of
setting his own opinions against tradition and Scripture as a
whole. But many Protestant scholars too, beginning with Luther's
colleague Melanchthon, have shared this evaluation and regarded
The Bondage of the Will as untenable both from a theological
and from a philosophical point of view. Misled by his fiery
temperament, Luther allegedly indulges in arbitrary philosophical
speculation and strays from the main lines of his own theology.
One must then attribute to Luther's stubbornness his own evaluation according to which only this work and the Large Catechism
are worthy of being preserved for posterity.

There are also many other frameworks in which the comparison of Luther and Erasmus has been made. Erasmus has
been seen, for example, as a new Pelagius whom Luther, schooled
in the Augustinian tradition, handles with his master's weaponry.[5]
Here the clash is between an idealism which finds the point of
contact between God and man in the will listening to the voice
of reason, and a Christian "realism" which stresses man's sinful
corruption and the sovereignty of God's grace. According to
still another frequent interpretation, Erasmus represents a Thomistic critique of Luther's Ockhamistic theology. Here the debate
is between the effort to create a synthesis of nature and grace,
reason and faith, human and divine, and the view that God and
man are separated by a chasm which only God in his inscrutable grace can bridge.

The debate has also been described as an expression of the
differences between two profound biblical scholars in the interpretation of specific texts.[6] Opposing each other are two one-

sided interpretations of Scripture. Although both seek to be
Christ-centered and obedient to divine revelation, they are
driven by the pressure of the situation into one-sided emphases.
According to this approach, the polemical elements of the dialogue have no significant content and reflect only a specific
ecclesiastical tension. The discussion is placed in its proper context when it is viewed as a phase in the long history of biblical exegesis.

In the Crosscurrents of Tradition

Regardless of the different ways of appraising the dialogue
between Erasmus and Luther from theological and philosophical
viewpoints, there is general agreement on one point: the problem of free will remains an open question to be solved by suc-
ceeding generations. The grounds presented by Erasmus in
defense of free will have proved to be untenable, and the logical
conclusion of Luther's position has been shown to be fatal-
istic determinism.

An interesting example of how the figures of Erasmus and
Luther look to a modern investigator of human nature is afforded
by an anatomy of the dialogue by Hobart Mowrer,[7] an American psychologist. He claims that in view of later developments
the discussion leaves the problem of free will entirely unsolved.
It bequeaths to the future only a disordered nest of difficulties.

According to Mowrer, many current analyses of culture indicate that man is becoming more and more optimistic about his
efforts to obtain mastery over his environment and at the same
time more and more pessimistic about the possibilities of obtaining mastery over himself. In the same decades in which men
have been able to achieve amazing scientific accomplishments,
the divisions between men and the experience of the sickness
of society have increased. These analyses have also made clear
that the simultaneity of the two contrary trends is not accidental.
The same basic endeavors which have led to an unforeseeable
rational control of nature, when directed to man himself, have
been the source of helplessness, confusion, resignation, and de-

spair. The law of cause and effect, applied as a universal principle to the world of nature, has proved to be a fruitful postulate, but applied to man himself it leads to a questioning of human worth, of human autonomy and responsibility, of man's whole identity.

Mowrer sees the fragmentation of man in Western culture as an expression of the same inability to deal with the problem of free will which is evident in the whole theology of the Reformation and particularly in the debate between Erasmus and Luther. In this respect the Reformation has bequeathed to the modern world a fateful legacy, forcing it into the alternatives of superficial moralism and a determinism eventuating in despair.

Western Christian thinking before the Reformation, Mowrer continues, held human responsibility to be twofold. Man is capable of both good and evil. If he chooses good, he is rewarded, and if he chooses evil, he is punished. Man's salvation or perdition is bound to his decisions between good and evil. This ethical system was based in many respects upon sound reason and everyday experience, but the church had gradually begun to abuse it, subordinating it into the service of its own striving for power. Erasmus, a man deeply conscious of moral responsibility, was concerned with the condition of life in his church. He raised a protest against the abuse and demanded that the church purge itself by returning to its origins, *ad fontes* ("to the sources"). By publishing the Greek text of the New Testament, Erasmus directed the church to its true authority, the basis on which the reform was to be conducted. For this reason Erasmus at first looked with favor upon Luther's endeavors, until as a man of reason and balance and as a humanist he gradually came to perceive that Luther was driven by irrational forces which inevitably led to moral irresponsibility.

Erasmus's book attacking Luther and Luther's reply to it have determined to our day the nature of both theological and popular discussion on freedom of choice and moral responsibility. Coupling Luther with Calvin, Mowrer claims that Luther in his dialogue with Erasmus represents clear determinism. To Luther man is responsible in only one respect. He is capable of choosing evil, and for that choice he is responsible. Having made this choice, man cannot free himself from the bondage he has brought upon himself but must wait helplessly for God's inscrutable act of grace. This position destroys the logic of the whole traditional theology which was founded on the twofold choice and stressed man's capability by his good works to take the first steps toward salvation. Erasmus defended this logic in adhering firmly to human freedom and responsibility in the choice of both good and evil.

Thus Protestant thinking, pursuing Luther's footsteps, has led to tragic results chiefly because it has destroyed the classical Christian legacy concerning man's responsibility. Christendom before the Reformation had proclaimed that the divine confronts the human as a call to ethical responsibility, and it had developed effective pastoral methods for unraveling the skein of personal guilt and bad conscience. This tradition was broken where Protestantism gained ground, and people were thrown into deep moral confusion. Although severe criticism of the Protestant ethic arose within Protestantism itself, as in the case of Kierkegaard, these strictures remained theoretical and negative in character, and inwardly fragmented people in the Protestant churches were left without care.

The inner fragmentation and moral confusion gradually drove people into the waiting rooms of the physicians. The medical profession had to take over the task of soul care neglected by Protestant theology. The inner moral and religious brokenness of men confronted the world of medicine with both somatic and psychic symptoms which were then portrayed as mental disturbances, nervous breakdowns, hysteria, neuroses, and so forth. The situation in which medical therapy had to provide help for people neglected by Protestant soul care is described in the autobiography of Sigmund Freud, the pioneer of this therapy: "In every larger European city crowds of neurotics were on the move, whose number seemed further multiplied by the way in which they hurried, with their troubles unsolved, from one physician to another."[8]

This therapy stretched out its hand to the confused and fragmented people but did not provide the expected help. Particu-

larly the therapeutic work based on the foundation laid by
Freud is dominated by the same spirit of determinism which
finds expression in Luther's *Bondage of the Will*. In fact, Mowrer argues, Freud agrees in principle with Luther that man is
helpless to save and cure himself. Freud and Freudian therapy
differ from Luther, however, in not holding man responsible
in any sense, not even for choice of evil. Such therapy seeks
to cure man from the confusion created by the Protestant ethic
by freeing him from all responsibility. Man is in no way account-
able for the condition which has driven him to seek care. In
the framework of this type of therapy it is impossible to speak
at all about man's guilt.

Thus Luther's *Bondage of the Will,* according to Mowrer,
expresses a deep current of Western thought, the effort to set
man free from the divine call to confession of personal guilt and
sin, which Christendom had heretofore sounded. To be sure,
Luther did not set forth his determinism in order to lead men
into arbitrary freedom and moral irresponsibility but to bind
them to the divine will. By its own inner pressure, however, this
view breaks that bond and is led to deny man's responsibility in
his relation both to God and to fellowmen.

From Luther's concept of man as thoroughly corrupt and helpless it is but a short step to the Freudian view of man as morally
confused and mentally ill, in need of the kind of care in which
man is not condemned but understood, in which he is freed from
the feeling of guilt by being helped to see that the causes are in
circumstances, not in himself. This psychological determinism
declares man's freedom from moral responsibility, claiming that
all human behavior is tied with iron bonds to the natural law of
cause and effect. Mowrer himself shares in putting the blame on
circumstances when he affirms that the Freudian view leads to a
still more fatal human fragmentation than does Protestant determinism. Luther's *Bondage of the Will* called man in all his bondage to seek God's grace, but deterministic psychology drives him
into the merciless world of scientific laboratories.

In the light of the data to be presented, Mowrer's portrayal of
the meaning of the dialogue between Erasmus and Luther will

prove to be one-sided. Yet it contains an important insight in its view of the dialogue as a manifestation of a continuing state of commotion which has its sources in the depths of Western culture. Strongest is the stream of idealism[9] which springs from these sources. While diverse currents have appeared in this stream, it is possible to speak in one respect of a single stream of idealism moving in one direction. A central thought impelling the development of Western culture has been the view of man as the product of a divine reality and nurtured by a divine ideal. The divine nature of man has been conceived in many different ways, but common to all types of idealism is the emphasis on the divine basis and goal of human existence. Inherent in man and in the reality surrounding him is something divine, and to share in it is the basic prerequisite of growth into humanness and of being man. This divine element is the reality of realities. It contains the basis on which human existence is to be built and the ideal for which it is to strive. Man's nobility and worth are in his divinity, and this is also what makes him a morally responsible being. The presence of the divine in man enables him to distinguish good from evil. The decisive thing about being a man is the choice between the good which conforms to the divine ideal and the evil which is opposed to it.

The whole tradition in the midst of which the dialogue between Erasmus and Luther took place had grown out of the efforts to blend Christianity with the idealism most resplendently expressed in the Greek spirit. There were efforts to identify idealism with Christianity and efforts to show that Christianity was the fulfillment of idealism, that it clarified the divine ideal and provided power for its realization. According to other interpretations, Christianity supplanted idealism as the only true mediator and fulfiller of divine revelation. In each case, however, the self-evident starting point was the idealistic view that the divine constitutes the objective and absolute ideal and goal for the human.

Both Erasmus and Luther grew up in the tradition which sought to blend idealism with Christianity, and both were well educated to discern its diverse currents. Each in his own way was also deeply disappointed at the way in which his generation had taken care of the heritage. Both were convinced that the preservation of the heritage was approaching its limits and that a radical renewal, in terms of a return to the original sources, was necessary. Both sought the springs of renewal primarily in the Bible, and both committed themselves wholeheartedly to the study and translation of the Bible.

These two men who never met each other face to face came gradually to perceive through their literary discussions that they were caught up in deeper currents than either had originally expected. Erasmus was frightened by the whirlpools, for year by year he became ever more convinced that the main stream was flowing in the right direction. There were crosscurrents because the main stream had become blocked, giving way to other streams. Erasmus was convinced that the crosscurrents would become quiet when the main stream of tradition resumed its power. Luther, on the other hand, perceived with increasing clarity that the crosscurrents were a sign of ever stronger whirls in the stream of tradition. Luther began to doubt the validity of the original starting points of the tradition, to question the synthesis of idealism and Christianity which that tradition had sought to create.

It is therefore no surprise that Erasmus begins to accuse Luther of destroying what is most precious in the tradition.[10] In speaking about the corruption of human nature and the disability of the human will, Luther is attempting to shake the very foundations upon which tradition rests. According to Erasmus, when Luther says that man has no merits, that even his pious actions are sinful, that man can do as little for his salvation as clay in the hands of the potter, that everything he wills and does is subject to absolute necessity, he is denying the operation of the divine in man. Luther thus shatters the view of man as divine which is the cornerstone of both the humanistic and the Christian heritage. In making such statements Luther has strayed into irresponsible exaggerations. Erasmus cannot understand how Luther can mean what he says. Luther's nominalistic and deterministic overstatements show that he has lost completely the capacity for objectivity.

Luther, for his part, retorts with a sharp refusal to admit that the assertions to which Erasmus refers are exaggerations resulting from a passionate temperament or from the tensions of the situation. At the same time he acknowledges Erasmus's perceptiveness in observing that the issue concerns the shaking of the foundations of tradition. He concludes his reply by praising the clarity of Erasmus's insight: "You alone, in contrast with all others, have attacked the real thing, that is, the essential issue. You have not wearied me with those extraneous issues about the papacy, purgatory, indulgences, and such like, which are trifles rather than serious issues. You and you alone have seen into the heart of the matter and placed the knife to the throat."[11] And just as Erasmus sees in Luther an unbalanced subjectivist who allows his preconceptions to lead him into errors and exaggerations, so Luther sees in Erasmus a bookworm, a petrified traditionalist, a pillar of salt staring into the past.[12] In one of his table talks Luther remarks that this staring backward has made Erasmus so blind to what is taking place around him that he looks at creation in the way a bull looks at a new gate. Thus Erasmus does not see the approaching dawn of life in which creation will appear in its original splendor.

So these two men relate themselves in completely opposite ways to the crosscurrents which they experience. Erasmus seeks to withdraw from the situation,[13] for he regards it as something transitory. He wishes to concentrate on the kind of constructive research whereby contact can be made with the original sources of tradition. Erasmus wishes to remain outside the controversies of the Reformation, for he feels that they approach renewal from a wrong direction and neglect the constructive study and education which alone make genuine renewal possible.[14] Luther, on the other hand, throws himself ever more decisively into the crosscurrents, convinced that the issue concerns not mere ripples on the surface but confrontation with deep streams crossing each other.

Luther begins to suspect that the tradition contains elements which are in irreconcilable contradiction to one another. The treatise by Erasmus indicates to Luther that the traditional theology leads to misleading alternatives and unessential problems. In his reply Luther makes an impassioned effort to detach himself from traditional questions which to him do not have essential importance. He reaches forward toward new questions.

Manifestly embittered by the injurious effects which tradition has had upon his own spiritual growth, Luther feels that his whole being is questioned when he comes face to face with a man who has experienced something of the same crisis and who yet continues to move within the alternatives furnished by tradition. Otherwise it would be difficult to understand why Luther would launch such a furious attack on a little book casual in nature and defending in a one-sided and popular fashion the lofty philosophical tradition of scholastic theology.

Luther's fury is directed primarily at the tone of Erasmus's writing[15] and at his choice of problems. He cannot understand how Erasmus can deal coolly and as an objective observer with burning questions issuing out of the depths of existence. Luther also rejects passionately the attempt of Erasmus to lure him back into the sphere of traditional theological discussion. He refuses to adjust himself to presenting merely new alternatives to old questions.

Erasmus tries to prove that there is nothing essentially new in the ideas presented by Luther. In his justified rebellion against the corruption prevailing in the church Luther has simply drifted into one-sided emphases. The thoughts which he sets forth have been present in the Christian tradition through the centuries. Their significance has not been denied, but detached from their proper contexts they have been seen as conducive to heresy and as inimical to sound and balanced theology, which is essential for the church. Erasmus tries to point out to Luther that some of his expressions about completely unconditioned grace and the bondage of the human will are such that consistent adherence to them leads unavoidably away from traditional Christian thinking and the theology of the church.[16] The deep agitation in Luther's reply shows that he himself has experienced profound uncertainty precisely at this point. In this respect Erasmus, with his insight into the heart of the matter, has struck Luther's Achilles' heel.

The question of the freedom or bondage of the will, in the form in which it has been debated by the indeterminists and the determinists through the centuries, is actually of no interest to Luther. In fact he questions whether this debate touches on any real problems. The free or bound will is the theme of Luther's reply to Erasmus only because the latter opened the discussion in these terms.

Erasmus's little book was intensely important for Luther because it challenged him to come to grips once more with the agonizing experience which had forced him to question the authority of his father, of his church, and of traditional religious thinking.[17] In Erasmus he confronted that side of his own being which accused him of arbitrary subjectivism and of an overestimate of his own experience and thought. He was keenly sensitive to this accusation at the particular time when he was writing his reply to Erasmus. Hardly ever had he been so alone as in the year 1525, when in the midst of the Peasants' Rebellion and its bloody aftermath he had to give account to himself and to others of the grounds of each position he assumed.

What *The Bondage of the Will* has to say must be examined primarily as an expression of a quest within Luther's own being and of his attempt to answer a question arising out of his own experience. He clarifies there the position which his experience of the divine-human encounter had led him to take toward what had traditionally been accepted as holy and endowed with divine authority.

Erasmus: Concerning the Divine Nothing Is Certain

Erasmus begins his study of free will[18] by affirming that of the many difficult questions raised by the Holy Scriptures none is as confusing and labyrinthine as this one. Philosophers and theologians through the ages have dealt with the problem without finding an adequate solution. Yet Luther attacks the issue with intense certainty, claiming in his principal writings of the year 1520 that free will is sheer illusion. Erasmus directs his criticism principally against Luther's presumed certainty and refuses from the outset to discuss the matter in the same spirit as Luther. He warns the reader against interpreting his dialogue with Luther in terms of an encounter between two gladiators. His purpose is only to single out one aspect of Luther's teachings and to examine it in the light of the Scriptures. Truth is not found by debating nor by defending one's own opinions as scriptural. The way to truth is careful and conscientious study of the Scriptures. Those who use the Bible to defend their own opinions are possessed by a dangerous certainty which makes objective study and judgment impossible.

For his own part, Erasmus considers the insights of skeptics more dependable than those of fanatics. He stresses, however, that he follows the skeptics only to the limits prescribed by the authority of the Bible and of the church. He declares his willingness to subject his own views to the decisions of the church whether or not he understands what the church prescribes.

Erasmus wishes to make clear from the beginning that he regards as unchristian the air of certainty manifest in Luther's writings. He confesses that he himself has no certain opinion in the traditional controversy on the freedom of the will. His only argument is that Luther has not convinced him of the total lack of freedom in the human will. In all other respects he continues to be a learner, admitting that he may be mistaken even if he has correctly understood Luther. He wishes to analyze rather than judge, to study rather than present dogmatic views. He announces his readiness to learn from anyone who can offer more accurate and reliable knowledge than he possesses. Erasmus regards the whole present discussion as useless. What prompts him to write is deep concern over the way in which Luther presents his views. He is disturbed by Luther's unwillingness to carry on a discussion in the spirit of learning and by the blind confidence in one's own opinions evident in Luther's writings. Erasmus is horrified by Luther's method of belittling tradition and the views of others and of depending only on his own inspiration.

As a scholar devoted to continuous learning Erasmus is concerned with Luther's air of certainty. But above all he cannot understand how Luther as a theologian with profound knowledge of the Bible can display such a spirit. To Erasmus it is incontrovertible that the Bible contains many things into which God does not want man to delve, matters which show the majesty of divine wisdom and the weakness of man's understanding. God's judgments are incomprehensible, and his ways past finding out. Man should not strive to participate in the councils of God. He should abandon the attempt to explain matters which transcend his rational capacity. Erasmus cannot understand how Luther as a theologian can concentrate chiefly on those very questions which the Bible wishes to preserve as divine mystery.

According to Erasmus, the discussion should center upon questions pertaining to man's salvation, the questions which the Bible calls upon man to investigate. In this perspective the Scriptures speak with unquestionable clarity: "If we are on the road to piety, we should continue to improve eagerly and forget what lies behind us; if we have become involved in sin, we should make every effort to extricate ourselves, to accept the remedy of penance, and to solicit the mercy of the Lord, without which neither the human will nor its striving is effective; for all evil let us consider ourselves responsible, let us ascribe all good to Divine Benevolence alone, for to It we owe even what we are; and in all things must we believe that whatever delightful or sad happens to us during life, God has caused it for our salvation, and that no injustice can come from Him who is by nature just, even if something should befall us which we deem undeserved; nobody should despair of forgiveness by a God who is by nature most merciful. In my opinion, it used to be sufficient for Christian piety to cling to these truths."[19]

To Erasmus it is obvious that Luther cannot be serious in saying that "free will is a mere name behind which there is no reality, for it is not in the power of any man to project anything good or evil."[20] Such an allegation, Erasmus exclaims, opens the gates to all kinds of godlessness. Most men live in ignorance and under the domination of the flesh. People have a tendency toward unbelief and all manner of evil. Luther's words pour oil on the fire. The Scriptures do not teach us to speak presumptuously to such difficult and complex questions.[21] Even though there were

something justifiable behind Luther's assertion, he shows irresponsibility in presenting such a thought publicly, for thus he is only
leading people astray from the path of salvation. It is not only
improper but actually dangerous and corrupt to debate questions of this kind in public. Erasmus concludes his preface by
saying that it is a waste of time and reason to wander into the
labyrinths to which Luther's arguments lead. One should therefore neither deny nor defend Luther's teachings. Erasmus remarks
finally that, while his preface may have been too wordy, what
he has said here is more important than the debate itself.

In the main body of his presentation Erasmus seeks to show
that the traditional Christian understanding of the nature of the
divine-human encounter is scriptural and that Luther's arguments about the corruption and bondage of the human will are
contrary to the whole heritage of Christian thought as well as
to the Bible. To the theme of the present study these analyses
by Erasmus as well as Luther's arguments in rebuttal have only
secondary importance. But in the structure of the main section
of Erasmus's presentation are features worth noting. In it appear
the contours of Erasmus's conception of the content of the Bible,
and it is clearly on this basis that Erasmus questions not only
this or that argument but the whole experience from which
Luther proceeds.

The structure of Erasmus's presentation shows that he is a
theologian of revelation.[22] He regards the Bible as the only source
of divine revelation. God unveils his true being in the person
of Christ. The Bible must therefore be studied in the light of
the spirit of Christ. The significance of the incarnation of Christ
is apprehended through growing penetration into the Holy Scriptures. In Christ the Bible becomes filled with the spirit of God.
The Scriptures thus have unique importance as the most per-
fect vehicle of divine revelation. The Scriptures are the ground
on which the saving action of the triune God confronts man.
To Erasmus divine revelation is found only in the writings of
the Bible, inspired by the Holy Spirit.

Particularly fundamental in Erasmus's interpretation of the
Bible[23] is the emphasis that the Scriptures share in divine mystery.

Theological research cannot penetrate the divine mystery both concealed and revealed in the Bible. The biblical exegete must acknowledge the limitations of his work. The purpose of biblical interpretation is to draw a man into a continuing interaction with the divine revelation contained in the Scriptures so that God's own speech and God's own spirit may make an impact upon him. In the Bible are pure divine words issuing from the depths of God's heart. When the Bible is approached with humble reverence, this divine speech touches man in an incomprehensible and verbally inexpressible way. Thus man comes to deal with the Spirit of God which distinguishes between good and evil, the mind of the spirit and the mind of the flesh, the divine spirit and the human letter.

The proper task of the student and interpreter of the Bible is to be a servant of divine revelation. In this task one must beware above all the setting of oneself above the word of the Bible. Only an interpretation obedient to the scriptural word leads to a confrontation with divine revelation. Erasmus is convinced that a theologian performs best this task as servant by following the critical methods of philological research. In this way the scholar is best equipped to overcome the temptation to set his own opinions in the place of the divine revelation. Severely critical biblical research leads to a theology which is obedient to revelation and remains its servant. Research of this kind conforms to the spirit of the Bible and to the doctrine of Christ, the *philosophia Christi*. This spirit also makes the scholar obedient to the church in which the divine mystery and revelation contained in the Bible is cherished and proclaimed. Thus the view of Erasmus has the character of church-centered theology of revelation.

Adhering to this basic view, Erasmus is led to deny all thought and speech of the divine which takes place in the spirit of certainty. Erasmus sees pride, even hubris, in a theologian who fancies that he can penetrate the divine mystery. He characterizes as "affirmative" the kind of theology which seeks to be normative in interpreting divine revelation.[24] Such a theology is in fact opposed to God's revealing action, for it replaces divine revelation with theological propositions. Erasmus holds in high regard the Greek academic philosophers who preferred to discuss matters unpretentiously rather than to present allegedly certain affirmative propositions.

In speaking about "affirmative" theology Erasmus does not refer to the Scholastics but to those theologians in the Christian tradition who have taken up theology in order to present their own opinions instead of the divine revelation in Christ. He remarks sharply that the trait by which these theologians can usually be recognized is that they have little factual knowledge but ample talent for showmanship. It is obvious that Erasmus sees Luther drifting toward the affirmative theological approach, for he begins his presentation with a warning against speaking in a spirit of certainty about divine reality and stresses the concealed nature of this reality. In his reply Luther takes up these two ideas at once, for here Erasmus questions radically the authenticity of Luther's whole being and thinking.

Luther: Nothing Is More Disturbing than Uncertainty Concerning the Divine

Luther begins the main presentation of his reply by declaring that the Christian life is impossible without certainty.[25] A Christian must create for himself a strong assurance and then confess and defend it without allowing anything to tempt him away from holding his ground. The divine Spirit is not a skeptic, and what this Spirit writes on the human heart has to do not with doubts and opinions but with matters of life that are more certain than all sense experience. In the same breath Luther also denies Erasmus's conception of the Bible and of the nature of divine revelation. He claims that the Bible is bright and clear and that divine revelation creates certainty, not uncertainty.

Just as Erasmus renounced decisively the spirit of certainty, so Luther announces from the outset his refusal to carry on the discussion in the way Erasmus suggests or to deal with his kind of questions. Luther argues that Erasmus's conception both of the relation between the Scriptures and experience and of the relation between revelation and reason shows him to be a skeptic who regards doubt to be the most reliable approach to life and reality. To Luther the acceptance of this starting point would mean an acknowledgment that the questions with which Erasmus deals are truly of vital importance. This Luther denies, claiming that the starting point selected by Erasmus leads to a discussion which evades the kind of questions with which the Scriptures are primarily concerned.

As noted above, what disturbed Erasmus most was Luther's air of certainty. According to Erasmus, the fundamental trait of a Christian is humble uncertainty. A Christian must admit that from the viewpoint of his experience and reason the Bible and the divine revelation it contains are unclear. Certainty of opinion or stance shows that a man is relating himself to reality with pride, and pride leads a man astray, whether he is facing divine revelation or the world of experience. It is this line of thought that indicates to Luther that Erasmus evades the urgent questions which the Scriptures call us to discuss. According to Luther, uncertainty is not humility but cleverly masked pride. Uncertainty becomes a place of refuge in which a man seeks to be protected from the flames of the most terrifying issues of life. The twin sister of doubt is not humility but pride. He who seeks to prove that all human experience is basically uncertain and that doubt is the only true approach to reality is actually defending his right to retain the positions and formulations which he has chosen as his starting point.

Luther seeks to show that Erasmus's own position is no more impartial and objective than the one which Erasmus has regarded as false dogmatic certainty. Luther asks Erasmus, "Why, then, do you advance the certain proposition: I do not accept certain propositions?"[26] Luther alleges that Erasmus in his preface performs a trick of legerdemain by which he tries to cover the fact that he too represents a definite conviction rather than purely objective views. In describing the content of divine revelation Erasmus sets forth his own conception of the nature of human experience. His basic position manifest in the discussion on certainty is also expressed in his view of the nature of divine revelation and the place which he assigns to the Bible.

This is Luther's view of Erasmus's basic position. Erasmus regards man as being above all a disciple of reality. Ideas and concepts are to be accepted or rejected according to the principle of whether they are in accord with experience derived from reality, that is, whether they are empirically verifiable. Man must train himself to learn constantly from reality. The more deeply man shares in objective reality, the less will be the danger of subjective arbitrariness. Reality contains the law and the ideal which teach man to realize true humanness.

In the light of the experience obtained in this school of reality, divine revelation has for Erasmus the nature of hiddenness, and the Bible is unclear.[27] Contained in the Bible is divine revelation transcending the reason and experience of the human individual. In accepting or rejecting the Bible he accepts or rejects the divine authority inherent in it. But the Bible and the divine revelation which it contains do not confront a man on the level at which he is a disciple of reality. To human experience and reason, divine revelation is unclear. The Bible opens itself only to a man who is willing to abandon the measures of experience and reason as he stands before divine revelation and who submits to obedience to divine authority.

Erasmus's view of man's essential being as a subject in training for objectivity, a disciple of reality, enables us to understand why he so firmly denies all certainty.[28] Human experience is by its very nature uncertain. The most dangerous enemy of growth into humanness is false certainty. When a man barricades himself behind his own subjective views and endows his own individual experience with highest certainty, he becomes blind and deaf to the teaching of reality. Subjective certainty prevents a man from learning that objectivity to which reality educates him. The greater the objectivity to which a man is trained, the less he is prisoner of his own subjective experience. The firmer the hold of objective reality upon a man, the more uncertain his subjective experience proves to be. If man's experience as a disciple of reality shows the danger of sure convictions to his growth as a human being, their harmfulness is even more evident in his dealings with divine revelation. In confronting the divine, man must confess his total uncertainty and in submissive obedience to the divine give up his dependence on human experience. Man's subjective experience in facing the divine is altogether untrustworthy, and his search for objectivity must also be subjected to guidance by divine revelation. A theology subservient to this revelation must therefore firmly deny any appeal to a man's own experience and convictions. A theologian who serves in transmitting divine revelation must break radically with his own subjective experience and his personal opinions and make way for divine truth alone.

Luther replies: The uprooting of sure convictions means the destruction of what is most essential to Christianity. A Christian and theologian who agrees to break with his own experience and his own convictions is completely adrift. Experience alone makes a theologian, *sola experientia facit theologum.*[29]

The Divine Authority of Human Experience

Characteristic of Luther, particularly in the polemical writings of the Reformation, is to present in the same breath grounds for his position from both the Bible and everyday experience.[30] This feature is evident throughout his reply to Erasmus. He affirms in numerous contexts that even the language of traditional theology is utterly foreign to the living speech of the Scriptures as well as to the vernacular now in use. He goes so far as to say that every man, even a little child, is enabled by his own experience to speak more "scripturally" than traditional theology about the presence of the divine in human life.[31] He claims also that every intelligent man perceives the absurdity of the idea of man's free will. Man's own experience and his common sense lead him to see how contrary to the facts of life are many of the traditional theological constructs. Thus the same Luther who in some connections rages against reason and experience appeals in other connections to sound reason and experience. This position receives its classical expression at Worms when Luther re-

fuses to recant unless he is shown to be wrong by the Bible
and by rational arguments.

Luther's recurrent appeal simultaneously to the Bible and to
everyday experience has usually been interpreted in terms of
either revelation-centered or nature-centered theology. According to the former method of interpretation, Luther speaks in
such cases about experience and reason as enlightened by divine
revelation.[32] By this means Luther is said to show that the world
of experience contains elements which confirm what the Bible
proclaims as divine revelation. These elements thus play a
secondary role in Luther's theology. According to the latter
interpretation, on the other hand, these sayings have central
importance in Luther's thought. They are said to reveal Luther's
effort to break with the church's sacramentalism, often magical
and opposed to nature, and to prepare the way for a natural
religiosity in terms of direct experience of God. Thus Luther's
aim would have been to afford every man the possibility of confronting the divine in his own way, guided by the directives of
the Bible. This type of interpretation has often sought to find
in Luther's personal experience the material for portraying
authentic religious experience.[33] Thus many Lutheran thinkers
who have stressed the empirical nature of faith have used Luther's
religious experience as a model for constructing various "orders
of salvation" (ordo salutis), tracing step by step the path to be
followed into an understanding of divine revelation. While the
revelation-centered view makes the Bible the standard for evaluating the authenticity of experience, the nature-centered view
judges on the basis of life and experience what in the Bible is
divine revelation.

These are the unavoidable alternatives in interpreting Luther
if his theology is examined primarily as an attempt to discover
a new answer to the traditional question of the relation of divine
revelation and human reason, grace and nature. It is obvious
that Erasmus so understood Luther's basic aim. He therefore
seeks to show the inconsistency of Luther's appeal to both the
Bible and his own conscience and convictions. According to
Erasmus, Luther ought to understand that such a position is

untenable. If he acknowledges the Bible as divine revelation, he should admit the uncertainty of his own opinions and experiences. But if he declares his conscience and experience to be the seat of judgment which ultimately decides what divine revelation is about, then he should admit his denial of the divine authority not only of the church but also of the Bible.

Luther is stirred not so much by what is expressed in the lines of Erasmus's treatise as by what he reads between the lines. He senses that Erasmus is trying to deprive him of certainty in order either to get him to confess humbly that the methods and questions of the traditional theology represented by Erasmus are the only possible ones in discussing the relation between the divine and the human, or else to show to the world that Luther is a sectarian fanatic reveling in his own religious ecstasies. When Luther in his reply speaks on the one hand about the clarity of the Bible and on the other hand about the relation between divine revelation and human experience, his presentation is in many respects so artificial and confused as to exhibit the very inconsistency which Erasmus seeks to expose.[34]

Erasmus apparently touched a sensitive spot in Luther when he raised the question of the dangers of certainty. In the years immediately preceding the debate a comparatively unknown monk had become a public figure whose ideas and attitudes attracted worldwide attention. When a man's opinions and stances are caught in the beam of publicity and he must give account to himself and to others for their effects upon communal life—only then is the strength of character and convictions truly assessed. Such an inner crisis threatens to bring about either a gradual crumbling of personal convictions or else a convulsive tightening of one's hold on them.

Luther's rise into prominence takes place quickly and sharply. The tension between uncertainty and certainty is therefore particularly distressing. On the one hand he feels in these years a gnawing sense of deep uncertainty, and on the other hand his public appearances are often marked by utmost certainty. The treatise by Erasmus forces Luther back into the inner agony from which he had escaped into the fortress of definite theo-

logical views. Thus the ensuing debate tears open once more a
crucial issue with which he had struggled from the beginning.

The impelling motive behind Luther's thinking in *The Bondage of the Will* is a question which had agonized him for two
decades: What is the divine authority in life, and how can one
be obedient to it in the right way? This distressing question
arose first in the serious conflicts which he experienced in his
father's relation to him and in his relation to his father. The
vast dimensions of this question, however, did not become apparent until he endeavored to discover the meaning of true obedience
in his relation to the church.

Studies concerning Luther's monastery years have portrayed
them mainly as that period of his life when in the light of the
Scriptures he gradually became aware how far his church and
its theology had become estranged from their original sources.
According to this interpretation, conscientious biblical study
enabled Luther to find in the divine revelation contained in the
Scriptures the authority which he sought. On the basis of biblical
authority he then proceeded to show the church where its practice and theology were contrary to divine revelation.

Viewed in this light, Luther developed during his monastic
period into either a revolutionary rebel or an "obedient" rebel.[35]
When Luther is regarded as a revolutionary rebel, he is described
as a man whose fidelity to the Bible drove him into an inescapable
conflict with his church, a man to whom the corruption of the
church appeared so deep that the way of revolution remained
the only solution. On the other hand, when Luther is described
as an obedient rebel, he is said to have set forth in the light of
the Bible the best elements in the theological heritage of his
church. According to this interpretation Luther appealed to the
authority of the Bible, not in the spirit of a radical destroyer of
tradition, but as a renovator of the church who endeavored to
preserve the true values in its heritage.

These interpretations appear to contradict each other. Their
basic structure, however, is the same. Both examine Luther's life
primarily from a churchly and theological point of view. They
see Luther as concentrating during his developmental years on

an attempt to solve the problems of his church. In this endeavor he then matures into either a radical rebel or an obedient rebel.

But another type of approach may be made. The spiritual exercises and theological inquiries of the years in the monastery may be viewed as expressions of a basically human quest on the part of Luther.[36] When they are analyzed in terms of a search for an answer to the question of authority, a question which unavoidably demands an answer in every man's process of growth and which decisively affects that growth, then they take on a meaning quite different from that of the church-centered analysis. Through the church and its tradition Luther's life became part of the broad and many-sided nexus of human experience. He made contact with men, both of past generations and of his own time, who had experienced the vital importance of the same question which he faced. These contacts gradually brought the conviction that the questions which rose from within himself and from the milieu of his life were not imaginary but real. He also realized that solving them or leaving them unsolved involved the wholeness or fragmentation of his own being.

In this context he began to grasp the significance of his own individual experience. He perceived that more is involved than his personal experience. He found in the fabric of his life threads which extended into the whole wide network of human existence. Through the connections with humanity established by the church and the Bible, the question with which he was wrestling reappeared as infinitely more complex and difficult, but now he was united with the company of others engaged in the same struggle. Thus he gradually came to the realization that his own individual history was a battleground of the history of mankind.

We neglect some basic features of Luther's inner struggle during the monastery years if we view it only as a search for new authority, as a gradual transition from subordination to the authority of the church to obedience to the message of the Bible.[37] The Scriptures did not become authoritative for Luther primarily because he found in them answers to questions which the church had left unanswered or answered wrongly. The most important experience which he derived from the sacred writings was that they revealed to him the importance of his own personal development and life. In the light of the Bible he began to realize that the questions distressing his conscience were not subjective, arbitrary, and trivial, or actually morbid, as other men and often also his own conscience had alleged.

Luther found in the Scriptures the courage to defend his own innermost way of apprehending truth and the integrity of his own experience. The Bible became authoritative for him, because through it his life and experience took on new meaning and value. From it he obtained the insight that to ascribe divine authoritativeness to anything other than that which one has personally experienced as such is like the contempt of oneself, a breaking of the first commandment.[38] The sacred writings convinced him that his human experience had contained a confrontation with the divine and that in his dialogue with life he had listened to a divine word. In the light of the Scriptures it became clear to him that no greater tragedy can befall a man than to become separated from the depths of his own being and from the immediacy of life's message reflected there. He became aware that only by participating in a continuous dialogue with life could he remain obedient to the calling which life had bestowed upon him and to the divine word contained in this calling. Thus he trained himself to listen to what the divine word as the word of his life spoke specifically to him.

Thus the deepest issue in Luther's development during the years in the monastery was not growth into the kind of obedience to the Bible which was to lead later into either a revolutionary or a constructive renewal of the church. It was training into a new kind of obedience to his own calling in life, which was to lead later to an unavoidable conflict with the traditional authoritarian faith. Luther's monastery years made him not primarily a church-man nor a Bible-man but a man seeking a good conscience.

The setting up of the authority of the Bible over against the authority of the church, a feature of Luther's writings in the first half of the decade beginning in 1520, has often been construed in such a way as to neglect Luther's basically human struggle. Torn from this context, the key assertions of the militant years of the Reformation have been transformed into theological slogans fraught with momentous consequences.

When Luther emerged from the sequestered life of a monastery into the arena of public life,[39] he faced the growing accusation on the part of the church that his convictions were not only one-sided but actually heretical. He was charged with questioning the authority of the whole tradition of the church. Thus he suddenly perceived that his convictions had precipitated an unexpectedly intense battle of spirits, one that was to be fought on a much broader front than he had anticipated. In such a situation he was compelled to build fortifications behind which he could take shelter, if only to catch his breath. One such fortress was the motto The Bible Alone *(sola scriptura)*. He defended himself from the charges made against him by appealing to the Bible. He attempted to show that his own thoughts and methods were in agreement with the Bible, while the practice and doctrine of the church were in disagreement with it.

The fortress of biblicism, however, was not merely a refuge for an excommunicated member of the church. The whole communal setting of Luther's activity was built on a definite view of the nature of authority, which was the basis on which the church acted and taught. This was a community in which no one had the right to appear publicly or to teach in his own name. All appearance and teaching in public had to take place in the name of an authority to which the community ascribed divine jurisdiction. Although the conviction of the untenability of this authoritarian faith had caused the upheaval which suddenly transformed a hermit into a pivotal public figure, he had to be able to prove before the judgment seats of the community and the bar of public opinion that he was appearing and teaching in the name of an acknowledged divine authority.

Luther had the alternative of setting against the authority of the church another authority also acknowledged as divine, that of the state. He confronted a different kind of situation as he faced the secular government which the community regarded as ruling by divine right. For understandable reasons he could not use in this confrontation the traditional appeal to the authority of the church. Unless he was willing to submit completely to secular authority, he had to find some other authority, for public appearance in the community had to have divine authorization.

In this predicament Luther was literally between two fires. He had personally experienced the disastrous effects of the authoritarian faith so deeply that he had committed himself to a wholehearted search for ways of getting rid of it and of discovering a new kind of faith, a new foundation of life. In this quest he suddenly found himself in a quandary in which he must appeal to the same type of authoritarianism which he sought to escape. In this dilemma the Bible furnished the only authority which enabled him to speak in the name of God both to the church and to the state.

From another point of view Luther's appeal to the Bible was something that might have been expected. We have observed that Luther's inner development took place in close contact and dialogue with the Scriptures. He lived in them and they in him in such a way that it is difficult to distinguish what is Bible and what is Luther. On the one hand the Scriptures led him to a deeper knowledge of himself, and on the other hand this deepening self-knowledge opened new insights into the world of the Bible. In this perspective Luther's appeal to the authority of the Bible is as self-evident as that of a scientist to the data of his research.

The fact that in this sense Luther regarded the authority of the Bible as self-evident has often been obscured by interpretations which have found the ground for his position in some particular religious experience. It has been common in Luther research to posit in his personal life some special event, pivotal for the Reformation, which convinced him of the divine authority of the Bible and gave him the courage to set it up against all other authorities.

The allegations that Luther derived his conviction of the divine authority of the Bible from some inner confrontation with Christ or from some theological insight into a particular text of Scripture are not only arbitrary in the light of the available data but they also result in dubious theological constructs. They lead one to view the Bible and experience, the divine and the human, as two fundamentally different worlds which some religious experience or revelation must unite. In the light of such a positing of the problem, Luther is seen as pioneering a new connection between the two realities, either by pointing out a new way to religious experience or by furnishing a new theological key to the world of divine revelation.

Regardless of whether some scriptural experience of Christ or some form of biblical theology is held to be Luther's conception of divine authority, interpretations of this type are blind to the material which throws light on the basic human aspects of Luther's experience. They also lead to artificial formulations which claim that Luther replaced belief in the church with belief in Christ, a God-relationship mediated by the church with a direct God-relationship of personal faith, the divine authority of the church with the Bible as the only divine authority. If these interpretations are correct, then Luther's ultimate concern was not a renewal of faith but only a transposition of the object of faith. Luther's development into a reformer would have to be described as a gradual liberation from the many authorities of his church until he acknowledged only a single divine authority. He learned gradually to doubt the divine character of the authority of the church fathers, the councils, the church's leading theologians, and the pope, and to recognize only the Bible as divinely authoritative. But if such was the case, the question which Erasmus addresses to Luther remains unanswered: How can an individual theologian declare his own interpretation of the Bible to be the only one true to the Bible?

These interpretations approach Luther in the same way as Erasmus does. If Luther's assertions concerning the clarity of the Bible and the questionableness of the authority of the church are examined from the point of view of scholastic theology, it is hardly possible to avoid Erasmus's evaluation of them. It is his judgment that, when the logical conclusions are drawn from

Luther's statements, the result is an arbitrary religious subjectivism in which the connection with Christian tradition becomes
more and more remote. In replying to Erasmus's criticism Luther
has to cope with these questions of tradition and authority in
which he has already lost interest. If we nail him down to the
statements on which Erasmus concentrates and consider them
to be his basic teaching concerning the Bible as the only divine
authority, we are involved once more in the dilemma which
Luther struggled strenuously to escape. When Protestants construct their view of the church on the sole authority of the
Bible—in the sense of external authority—they are returning to
that very structure of the life of the church which Luther
experienced as stifling to human conscience. When the authority
of the Bible takes the place of the authority of the church or
when trust in individual religious experience takes the place of
churchly experience, there has been no structural change in the
relationship to authority.

We have underscored the natural and self-evident character
of Luther's adherence to the authority of the Bible in order to
set forth a point of view which has received scant attention in
Luther research: the Bible became Luther's authority chiefly
because it freed him from authoritarian faith as such. Both in
his own life and in the life of the church he had found this
faith to be oppressive to conscience. In battling for the authority
of the Bible he was battling primarily for the right to be
Martin Luther.

In arguing that the practice of the church is in contradiction
to the Bible Luther seeks to show above all that it is life-denying.
The church has drawn up countless regulations which conflict
with God's commands inherent in life. The church has constructed a language entirely different from people's everyday
language. The church regards celibacy as the highest ideal, while
life shows marriage and the family to be the basic structures of
community. In defending the Bible Luther is defending a nexus
of life which his own inner development, in a close interaction
with the Bible, has shown to be conducive to fruitful growth.
Welling up from the ground in which his life grows are springs

which liberate him to think, to feel, and to will in such a way as to lead him to construe all this as a confrontation with the divine.

In Luther's own being there occurred within the course of a few years a powerful renewal like the breaking up of the ice of winter. In the midst of it his thought and his speech blossomed forth in a way which amazed both himself and those about him.[40] To Luther himself this surge of life came as an incomprehensible surprise, and most of those in his immediate social environment considered it as something sick or even demonic. His innermost thoughts were labeled as heretical, his feelings immoral, and his will defiant of the will of God and of the authority of the church. The genuineness of his whole life and experience was thus called into question.

To Luther this meant that the Bible was also called into question, for the Bible had become an inseparable part of his being, the means by which he had experienced the transformation which amazed him and the others. In this perspective it was quite natural for Luther to speak in the same breath of the Bible and of his own experience. The famous assertion "Here I stand, I can do no other" shows that he is not impelled primarily by the effort to defend the authority of the Bible against the authority of the church, nor by the effort to prove that his own theological insights are true and scriptural, but by his feeling and conviction that what he has experienced is neither morbid nor demonic but an authentic experience of a promise inherent in life itself. In this light Luther's appeal to the authority of the Bible is a defense of the genuineness of his unique personal experience. It is thus a battle for the right of a man to be a man of conscience. When Luther declares that it is never good for a man to act against his conscience he is not defending his own subjective way of feeling or thinking nor what his own inner struggles have revealed to him to be the basic message of the Bible. He is battling above all for his right to be a man of conscience, a man who has the right to participate in life as a person, as a representative of his own particular experience, not merely as an anonymous student of reality, an object for manipu-

lation by communities appearing in the name of divine authority
and an instrument of their endeavors.

The question of the authority of the Bible and its relation
to the authority of the church is secondary for Luther as he
seeks to find an escape from the traditional authoritarian faith
and attempts to discover where and how the divine can become
a genuine authority in human experience. Primary is the fact
that Luther has experienced in his own being the life-destroying
nature of the traditional authoritarian faith. His rebellion against
it grows out of an outraged conscience, out of the conviction
that what confronts him in the name of divine authority is in
irreconcilable conflict with what he has experienced, in his
own being, as true. In seeking an answer to the question of true
authority Luther seeks to assess what in his own life is tenable
and genuine and what is erroneous and unauthentic, what is
divine humanness and what is human godliness.

Step by step his experience leads him to a deepening conviction that the blind alleys in which he has found himself,
whether in his own thinking or in his relation to fellowmen,
exist not only in himself but also in his community. Gradually
it also becomes clear to him that there is no way of getting
around these blind alleys. One gets into them not by misleading
approaches which hold sway in a community now and then but
by judgments and evaluations fundamental to his community
and held to be self-evident and divine.

Search for authentic life and search for God's word thus belong together in Luther's experience. In listening to the speech
and word of life or in becoming deaf to it, one is dealing with
the speech and word of God. In the mandates of life the divine
seeks authority over man. Especially in the most critical years
of the Reformation and in the years directly following them
the central theme of Luther's writings is that the church has
set itself in opposition to God's word. The intensity of his
concentration on this theme and the appeal to his own experience
indicate that his chief concern is not to show that the church
is in contradiction to some definite biblical norm or to some
specific theological formulation of divine revelation. The church's

opposition to the word of God consists above all in the fact
that it breaks off man's contact with life and with his own being
and thus suppresses man's conscience.

Luther claims that the foundation of the churchly forms of
life is authoritarian faith. Thus what the church under the guise
of divine authority seeks to realize and sustain makes a man
uncertain about everything that he has experienced within himself. In this way the church destroys man's basic confidence
in life. It denies man the right to put his roots into the soil of
his own being and to grow in his own life-calling into a person,
a being who has been called to discover for himself where in
his experience lie the divine promises and demands and where
they are endangered.

In speaking about neglect of God's word as the basic error
of the church Luther does not refer mainly to a slighting of the
Bible or of biblical proclamation in the worship of the church.
He believes that God's speech is most thoroughly suppressed by
the church's effort to uproot a man from the soil of his own
growth and to transplant him into the greenhouse of the church.
Nor is the monastic system, according to Luther, in opposition
to God's word because biblical study has shown him the difficulty
of finding a basis for it in the Bible but because the promises
taken and given there in the name of God are irreconcilable
with the promises inherent in life. God's word is silenced when
the divine groundwork of human life is replaced by some other
ground or nexus of life that is deemed better.

For Luther reverence for life and honoring God's word belong
inseparably together. This does not mean that the speech of life
as such is the speech of God, or that the word of life as such
is the word of God. It is as foreign to Luther to identify the
word of God with the Bible as to consider some inner word
issuing from experience as the word of God. Luther neither
seeks to supplant the authority of the church with the authority
of the Bible nor tries to weigh his own experiences, opinions,
and inner word versus the church's rich heritage of experience.

The true source of Luther's criticism of the church is not
found in experiences which show him that the church is in

conflict with its own scriptural premises, nor in experiences in which the contradiction between the teachings of the church and his own personal convictions proves to be irreconcilable. The source of the agitation which leads Luther to insist unsurrenderably that the church not only neglects but actually opposes the word of God lies deeper than is assumed in the interpretations that make him a champion of biblicism or of the liberty of an individual.

There are two main interpretations of Luther's double appeal to God's word and to conscience, evident at Worms and especially in his theology during the early years of the Reformation. On the one hand, the point of gravity in Luther's proclamation and theology has been posited in the idea that the word of God, here identified with biblical revelation, is incomprehensible without definite religious experience. On the other hand, Luther's effort is said to have been to show that the Bible alone must be the authority for a man's conscience. When the former line of reasoning is consistently pursued, it yields the conclusion that a man's conscience, enlightened by religious experience, becomes the basis for judging what in the Bible is God's word and what in man's experience is faith or unfaith. The criterion here is experience. The latter method results in regarding the Bible and its orthodox interpretation as the basis of evaluation. Here the criterion is the Bible and doctrine. Thus Luther has been regarded as either a religious subjectivist or a champion of biblical objectivism.

While it is apparent that Luther's labors in his own inner workshop take place, in a large measure, on the ground of his ecclesiastical and theological heritage, yet out of this forge emerge products which tend to break up the fossils of tradition. Thus the weighty research material which Lutheran theology has consigned to the alternatives of subjectivism and objectivism brings to light also the effort to abandon the entire subject-object formulation in examining the divine-human encounter.

This is indicated, for example, by the way in which Luther deals with Erasmus's arguments concerning the authority of the church and that of the Bible and their interrelationship. It is obvious from Luther's presentation that he is not stuck fast behind the fortifications of biblicism in which he had sought shelter in being suddenly compelled to explain the grounds of his faith to the spiritual and secular authorities of his community. It is strikingly significant that Luther, unlike Erasmus, does not protect himself with the armor of biblicism but bravely exposes his own agonized heart and being. In such a situation it would have been most tempting for him to confine himself to demonstrating first the absolute authority of the Bible and then the unbiblical nature of Erasmus's arguments. In keeping with the contemporary academic procedure it would also have been natural to point out first what texts were authoritative for the discussion, and for what reason, and then to prove that the inherent logic of these texts did not permit the interpretation given by his opponent. Especially when the opponent was a humanist such as Erasmus, to whom a return to the original sources and a revaluation of tradition in this light was the basic purpose of all research, it would have been in the nature of the case to concentrate on showing that the Scriptures are the church's original source and that Erasmus was inconsistent in adhering to the authority of the church itself.

In Luther's reply there is much to indicate the attractiveness of this temptation. In those sections of his reply in which he seeks to overcome Erasmus's interpretation of the Bible with his own, his presentation is often quite inconsistent and inclined to an arbitrary use of scriptural texts to support his own interpretation. When Luther seeks, like Erasmus, to prove his case by appealing to the Bible, his argumentation is as artificial as that of Erasmus. But this material, although arbitrary and artificial from the point of view of exegesis and logic, contains expressions which reveal the unimportance of the immediate settings and point to the true sources of Luther's attachment to the Bible. The whole structure of Luther's reply demonstrates his effort to detach himself from Erasmus's questions and to develop both a new method of discussion and new questions.

The Divine Nature of Human Authority

The difference between the basic approach of Erasmus and that of Luther becomes especially clear in their relation to tradition. Erasmus is wary of Luther's endeavors because he sees them as leading inevitably to an uprooting from the soil of tradition.[41] According to Erasmus, continuity in the rhythm of the generations and preservation of heritage can be realized only through submissive obedience to the divine authority which the church represents as steward of the mystery of divine revelation. If this authority is denied, as Luther appears to do, then the rhythm of the generations is broken, the prestige of tradition is shaken, and the result is arbitrary rebellion and subjectivism. From Luther's point of view it is precisely the traditional authoritarian faith represented by Erasmus that constitutes the most serious obstacle to a genuine continuity in the rhythm of the generations and makes for a perverted relation to tradition. The shackling together of the generations carried on by the church in the name of divine authority, the *successio* which it has constructed and maintains, is contrary to the divine promise contained in life itself, the promise which Luther has discovered from the Scriptures to be the only foundation of vital and true continuity.

We must bear in mind that Luther wrote his reply to Erasmus under conditions in which an appeal to the Bible's prophetic message of social justice and to the revolutionary nature of the gospel meant incitement to rebellion against the established social order.[42] Luther's writings dealing with the Peasants' Rebellion show how deeply this turbulence shook his innermost being and thinking.[43] His heart was in many ways on the side of the rebels, for he recognized in them the voice of his own soul. Just as he had experienced in the institutional church the injurious effects of the entrenched authoritarianism upon his own life and growth, so he saw the rebels as badly mangled by social structures built on the foundation of the same authoritarian faith. His sympathy was with those who were impatient with the established social structures.

But when in this situation—in a manner which proved to be tragic in many respects—he exhorted "the powers that be" to use all available means to strike down the rebels, many of his enthusiastic supporters turned their backs on him, convinced that he had forsaken the original aims of his reformation.[44] Yet he saw himself as serving the same revolutionary cause which had led him to attack the authoritarian faith of the church. In the commotion of the peasants this spirit of revolution exposed the injurious and destructive nature of the prevailing social structures. But while Luther calls for a radical reexamination of the alleged divine right of the traditional orders of social life and thought, he also sees the revolutionary movement as drifting into wrong directions, into religious fanaticism which rejects all churchly tradition and into rebellion which attempts to overthrow all established social orders.

These views of Luther's are in a sense a review of decisions made earlier under the pressure of specific situations, and they represent a rationalization of the position he had taken. Finding himself drawn suddenly into the limelight of publicity to explain to the ruling powers his doubts about the authority of the church, he had rationalized his position by appealing to the authority of the Bible. Now he set forth the doctrine of the divine authority of secular government to defend a position taken in the midst of social revolution and not altogether consistent with his total outlook. This rationalization, growing out of a specific situation, was in danger of becoming as fateful as the "scripture alone" principle, which had been designed to meet the exigencies of another specific situation.

In view of the factors contributing to the rationalization, however, it may also be seen as an expression not only of being determined by a situation but also of a quest for something new. Luther's conception of the secular government as divine is not a mere emergency measure, a modus vivendi, a rationalization of circumstances. It bears evidence of a radical quest growing out of his own experience.

The conception of the secular government as divine is placed in the wrong context if attention is not given to Luther's effort to find a new solution to the whole problem of authority. To conceive his statements on the divine nature of secular government as an attempt to support existing authority is as misleading as to interpret his appeal to the authority of the Bible as an attempt to replace the authority of the church by the authoriy of the Bible. Just as Luther's assertions on the divine nature of the Bible do not aim at elevating the Bible to be the highest tribunal in the life of the church, so in speaking about the divine authority of government Luther does not seek to absolutize the authority of the state. He rebels against the whole life-attitude which seeks to elevate some structure of life, whether the Bible or government, church or state, into a court which decides for men the basic issues of their life. He feels so deeply the damage done by this kind of attitude and faith that he finds himself in the role of a reformer.

In this perspective, when Luther speaks about the divine nature of secular government he is taking a stand against prevailing authoritarianism, the kind of divinization of established ecclesiastical and social structures which he questions. This does not mean that he considers respect for human authorities and obedience to them as obstacles to an encounter with the divine. On the contrary, the elevation of something from the common life to objectivity, civil authority, or tribunal, and the process by which this is done are of central importance in confronting the divine. Luther's criticism is directed primarily against the way human authority is used to represent the divine itself.

It is foreign to Luther to think of confrontation with the divine as taking place in situations in which the church or the Bible is set up as a special zone of experience representing divinity. It is just as foreign to him to regard some social system or network of earthly vocations as basic manifestation of the divine. The quest for the divine within such frameworks blinds man to the real presence of the divine in human life. Just as Luther studies the Bible chiefly as the book of life containing writings that are sacred because they awaken men to cherish what is most sacred in the basic web of life, and just as he evaluates the life and message of the church from the viewpoint of one thus awakened, so he also views social orders and secular government in the light of this comprehensive divine humanness.

It is noteworthy that Luther usually speaks of the divine nature of secular government in the same context in which he deals with the fourth commandment.[45] This has often been interpreted to mean that he derives the authority of government from the authority of the father. It is indeed obvious that Luther speaks in many connections about patriarchal authority in a way that stamps him as a child of his time. One may gather from his writings abundant evidence that he conformed to the thought pattern of his day in regarding the family, grounded on the principle of the father's authority, as a divinely established order. This data has been used to support a theology of the orders of creation,[46] which has obtained a strong foothold in the Protestant world. It has singled out some social structures, for example, monogamous marriage, patriarchal family, the nation as an organism, and some specific form of the state, and posited them either in the place of the Bible and the church or alongside of them as those areas of experience in which the divine confronts the human and which therefore have divine authority over the rest of experience. In the shadow of such interpretations attention has been diverted from data in which the grounding of the divine nature of government in the commandment to honor one's parents is presented in an entirely different way.

Data of this type is found especially where Luther deals with his relation to his father. He often seeks to point out to his father that there is both justification and obligation in his refusal to obey him. Attention must be given particularly to Luther's emphasis that the fourth commandment is to be examined in the light of the first commandment. Parents have no right to constitute themselves as their children's conscience or to require them to pursue goals set by the parents. The first commandment protects the right of the child to grow and develop into a unique person, a man of conscience. In the light of the first commandment a child has the right and the obligation to refuse to obey his parents, if in their own name or in the name of divine authority they command him to act against his conscience.

Yet according to Luther the fourth commandment is a basically important commentary on the first commandment. It establishes an organic relation between the commandments of the first table, which deal with confronting or evading the divine in words and thoughts, and the commandments of the second table, which speak of the same divine-human encounter in acts that take place where the paths of human life cross one another. Directly following the first table is the commandment to honor one's parents. It is a summons to reverence for all human life as it unfolds in both words and deeds, for in it the divine is present.

Luther also points out that this commandment reveals how divine humanness is realized or left unrealized, whether in words or in deeds, by the way in which life is received and in turn given to others. Most decisive in the encounter with the divine is what takes place in that basic interaction of human life in which men receive from one another and give to one another. Here the primary decision is made whether the soil of life will produce divine humanness or godless inhumanness. The fourth commandment deals above all with the cultivation of a life-orientation in which the word of life contained in human acts nourishes a receptive human being and enables him to grow to be the word of life for others.

The fourth commandment is a call to cherish and to hold in special honor that life-relationship and that interaction between human beings in which one man by virtue of his experience and status is the parent, guardian, teacher, judge, and so forth, of another man whose role is to receive, to be guided and instructed. These human relations are threads in the fabric of life and have decisive influence in shaping both words and deeds. In characterizing parental and governmental authority as divine, Luther stresses man's special responsibility in all exercise of power and authority. He points out what grave responsibility a man assumes when he represents the authority of the word of life.

When Luther describes the structures of life as "God's masks" (larvae dei)[47] he stresses their decisive importance in the realization of divine humanness but he does not declare human authorities as such to be divine. On the other hand, in unfurling the banner One Must Obey God Rather than Men, he focuses his attention on the quality and inner structure of these relationships of life. His purpose is not to proclaim some principle of equality which would invalidate all human authority.

In Luther's vocabulary the word *trust* has a central place. He sees human life as built on and realized through such confidence. The most tragic injuries to human existence occur when the basic trust is shattered. The promise inherent in life is tested in those forms of life together in which one man has authority over another. If man meets man in these relations in a way that negates his status as fellowman (the commandment to love one's neighbor), not only is injury done to oneself and to others and the common fabric of life torn, but a position of defiance is taken against the giver of life himself who has called men to be givers (the commandment to love God). In the relations of parent and child, giving and receiving, governing and being governed, life's circulation of blood is either promoted or obstructed.

Luther emphasizes the sanctity and divine nature both of the family and of society in general because they preserve the fundamentals of life. He does not raise the question whether some specific form of the family or of society is to be considered as a divine order of creation. He examines these structures from the point of view of fidelity to the basic groundwork of life. A major portion of Luther's theological works deals with the structure of the family, with the condition of the schools, with the exercise of power and the bearing of the sword, and with the use of money by the church and by secular society and its consequences for shaping human relations. The keynote of all these writings is a call to those who have special authority to recognize their special responsibility in the preservation of the essentials of life.

Luther never wrote a systematic theology or a dogmatics. He did not try to present any divine program or plan for human life. He made no attempt to create a system of theological concepts embracing all reality. His writings, especially *The Bondage of the Will*,[48] concentrate on the search for the all-important pivots on which life turns and which determine whether life develops into divine humanness or becomes dehumanized. This quest leads

Luther to emphasize that all relations of parent and child, teacher
and learner, leader and follower, judge and recipient of judgment, trainer and trainee, giver and receiver, ruler and subject,
healer and patient, binder and bound, and releaser and released,
have decisive importance in weaving the human fabric.

Man as Chosen by Life

In grounding the bondage of the human will in the basic web
of life, Luther is saying that man must face the inevitable fact
that life is fundamentally not of himself. The birth and growth
of human life consist in being chosen. How life is realized in those
relationships where man experiences his dependence on the
ground of his existence and of his fellowmen is of critical importance to the process of becoming a human being. In experiencing this dependence man makes the fundamental decision: will
he be open or closed to life, will he consent to living as chosen,
or will be choose another form of existence? This decision takes
place in the depths of man's being even before he consciously
adjusts himself to reality. In the experience of communion with
life, in which one either opens or closes himself to life, the main
direction of man's conscious behavior is predetermined. To the
degree that his basic decision is to be chosen by life and thus to
be open to reality, the will to be united with life's basic interconnections develops in man. To the degree that the decision is to
the contrary, the will to destroy the fundamental structures of
life is generated.

In saying that everything in life takes place by necessity,
Luther explains that necessity *(necessitas)* is not the same as
coercion *(coactio)*.[49] He means to say that man's conscious
behavior is not determined by an unavoidable conformity to
situations and circumstances but grows organically out of his
own being. Acts are not engendered fortuitously by the pressure
of various external conditions but emerge as the results of an
inner preparation. Reactions to life do not occur by accident or
by compulsion but grow out of a specific background, the basic
decision which man has made in the depths of his being.[50]

As man experiences life, his will is bound in the sense that he must either affirm life or deny it. His will must be either open toward growth in the basic web of life or closed and bent on destruction. In either case man is inescapably a free and willing being. In this sense all the activity of the human will is free. To be a man means volitional growth. A man grows in the direction of his will.

Distinctive of all genuine willing is that it cannot be changed by coercion. A man does not do good or evil against his will. If external compulsion drives a man to do something against his will, his will still opposes this action, and the more opposition the will encounters the stronger it becomes. If man's growth is organically united with the basic web of life, it cannot be forced into some other direction of growth. A life-denying will is likewise a genuine will, not one under compulsion. In neither case can a man change the direction of his will without changing his basic orientation to life.

Salvation in the sense of healing or wholeness of a human being is thus not something that man can achieve by his own efforts, for the core of his being, his true self, is not under his own sovereignty. Man experiences in the depths of his own being the presence of the divine.

According to Erasmus,[51] free will is the capacity of man to apply himself to those things that lead to eternal salvation or to turn away from them. Man lives before the promise of eternal life and the threat of eternal punishment, and he must choose between them. Luther argues that to hold such a view is to insult both God and man. Here both are conceived as beings without a will, beings that allow some factor outside themselves to determine their conduct. Both God and man are regarded as mere observers of reality. God sets up the alternatives and then determines his relation to man by the way in which man relates himself to them. Man seeks to discover his relation to God by observing what is rewarded and leads to salvation and what is punished and leads to perdition.

With this caricature of Erasmus's view Luther attempts to show that it implies an idolization of God and a dehumanization

of man. He writes, "Nor can reason come to any other conclusion. As she herself snores and makes light of the things of God,
so she thinks of God as snoring over them too, not using his
wisdom, will, and presence to act, separate, and inspire, but leaving to man the tiresome business of heeding or defying his grace
and anger."[52] Luther's analyses of the nature of the divine will
and of the human will, presented in this connection, may likewise
be caricatured, and his conclusions may be shown to be as untenable as those of Erasmus. He succeeds, however, in making one
thing clear: in debating about the will, the two men use the same
word but mean something entirely different.

Luther claims that Erasmus's analysis of the freedom of the
will does not pertain to the human will at all. Erasmus portrays
basic human action as taking place under the pressure of external
reality and within the alternatives which it imposes. This does not
deserve the name of will. Here various forces and laws drive man
in a direction determined by them. They compel man to perform
deeds of their choosing.

Such acts, which Luther designates as works of the law, have
their own place and significance in human life. Under the pressure of laws and of forces elevated by other men to the status of
objective realities, a man who is separated from the basic vitalities
and in conflict with the structure of life must nevertheless perform "good works," even against his will (the first use of the
law).[53] Luther describes such acts as dead works, for they are not
in reality a man's own works but acts which he is compelled to
perform. If the performance of such works becomes a man's way
of life, he becomes uprooted from the soil of life[54] and his conscience is dulled. This is what Luther means by hardening and
reprobation. The life which hardens man is that in which he cuts
himself off from his own being and conforms to some external
reality which he declares to be absolute and objective. On this
road a man is in danger of becoming a being without conscience
or will.

Luther detects in Erasmus's emphasis on the freedom of the
will the voice of a man who is free in the sense of being detached
from the vital connections of existence. Such detached liberty,

according to Luther, is bondage to "objective" reality which determines the course of a man's life. When Erasmus speaks of the freedom of the will, Luther hears a defense of a position achieved through dissociation from the basic web of life and made the standpoint for examining all reality. To Luther this means yielding to man's original temptation to seek mastery of the knowledge of good and evil.

Over against this view, Luther presents his thesis of life as governed by divine election and will. In describing man as a mount for which two riders contend[55] he gives expression to the tension between being united with the vitalities of human existence and being detached from them. By clinging to these vitalities and being bound to them a man is free to grow into an authentic human being. By isolating himself from them and withdrawing into his own world in which he seeks to control reality by his knowledge of good and evil, a man becomes the prisoner of the world which he has created.

Luther argues that Erasmus speaks of the human will as a will free in separation from the divine. He finds evidence for this in Erasmus's conception of the nature of commandments. According to Erasmus, the fact that life contains divine commandments indicates a confrontation between God's will and the free will of man. It would be irrational to issue commandments which could not be fulfilled. Erasmus also claims that everyday experience in human relations proves the same fact. Imperatives have an important place in everyday language. They show that human growth takes place in obedience to commandments.

To Luther these arguments show that Erasmus disregards entirely the world of divine and human willing. The use of imperatives in everyday language indicates something quite contrary to what Erasmus says. Imperatives do not express what may happen or does happen. That is expressed by indicatives. Imperatives as such do not presuppose that the commands can be fulfilled. Everyday language abounds in imperatives which cannot be fulfilled either by the one who commands or by the one who is commanded. Men issue commands to one another precisely because of this inability, not because the commanding changes men.

The abundance of imperatives reveals men's inability to preserve the vital relations to which the commands refer.

Imperatives lead a man to see where his growth has been disrupted. In them some basic vitality, some fundamental element in the structure of life, speaks its piece. Some vital thread in the fabric of life is about to break and calls attention to its plight through the imperative. The compulsive use of imperatives reveals the fragmentation of the basic vitalities.[56] On the other hand, life is experienced as being subject to imperatives in the sense that it is something given, something with which man is in dialogue. But present is the danger that life will remain unlived, its promise unrealized, its speech unheard, and its commands unfulfilled. Man is at the same time righteous and sinner, *simul justus et peccator*.

In his exegetical studies dealing with the Decalogue and the Mosaic legislation, Luther speaks of the twofold nature of these commandments and laws.[57] On the one hand, they reflect the election and the promise contained in the imperative *(mandatum dei)* which the people of Israel experienced to be the foundation of existence. On the other hand, the large number of the commandments and laws shows that the same people found in itself a tendency to escape from the election. Luther attaches special attention to the fact that both the Decalogue and the code of laws affixed to it are portrayed as having been given to a people that refused to be the elect one,[58] to live vis-à-vis the giver of life. In this sense the law is a later addition, as the New Testament expresses it. Thus, while the commandments and laws set forth the call to live as the elect people, they also expose the strong hold obtained on that people by the spirit of refusal, the spirit of the flesh.

In speaking about Abraham's obedience to the divine will Luther points out that the issue here is not the submission of a man's free will to a given command. Abraham as prototype of a man of faith is not an example of how this kind of obedience to a divine command receives a blessing. Abraham is not made righteous by his obedience, but he sets out on the road of obedience because he is righteous, because he lives in dialogue with life. The life story of Abraham exemplifies the inner and outer conflicts experienced by one who lives as elect.[59] He is an example of a man who does not create his own world on the basis of his own knowledge of good and evil but who consents to grow in dependence upon the election and the promise of life. Experience of this election and promise impels Abraham to action. He becomes aware of stirrings within himself which cause him to doubt the views and attitudes which he has shared as a member of a specific social group. The Scriptures do not praise Abraham as the father of believers in the sense that his faith and action are to be copied. The story of Abraham is a call to openness to life's election and promise. In Abraham no way of believing or living is elected as divine, but in him life is shown to contain divine election.

Luther considers Erasmus's emphasis on free will as tragic particularly because it results in a denial of the presence of this election in life. In his reply Luther argues repeatedly that Erasmus is under the spell of the view of God presented in Aristotle's philosophy of nature, according to which the divine is realized in the human under specific presuppositions. To Luther the basic error is not that the concept of nature determines both the concept of God and the concept of man. He applies to Erasmus the same criticism as he does to Thomas Aquinas, whom he describes as being dominated by the spirit of Aristotle. The basic error of Thomas Aquinas, says Luther, is that he views the encounter between the divine and the human as conditioned by certain presuppositions. "The conditioning brings about all the misfortune."[60]

Luther insists that to place conditions upon the confrontation between the divine and the human is to refuse to live as elect. Here man himself chooses what elements in reality are to be regarded as most real, thus building his life on a foundation of his own choosing. Human action is regarded as the starting point of being human (*operari sequitur esse*, "being follows action"). Man is conceived as a being who is what he makes of himself. Faith thus becomes unavoidably a human act, an act by which man himself creates the divine. Luther's own emphasis is that faith is not the product of human thinking or the result of human activity. Faith is a reality in which man exists before he does anything (*prius est autem esse quam operari,* "being precedes action").[61]

With his emphasis that the connection between God and man is created by the word alone *(solo verbo)* and by faith alone *(sola fide)* Luther focuses attention on the inseparable relationship to the divine implied in the very fact of being a man. The starting point in speaking about the encounter with the divine cannot be an abstract God and an abstract man but must be a concrete linkage whereby God lives in man and man in God. God, the word, faith, and man are inseparable realities.

The Divine Word Contained in Man's World of Reception[62]

One of the words which Luther uses most frequently is *listening.* He describes man as a listener to reality. Man listens and responds. An animal does not speak because it does not hear the speech of life. Only man lives in dialogue with life. This dialogue does not concern merely the hearing of words or the responding with words. It concerns a listening, to which one is either obedient or disobedient. Man's whole life is in this respect a word, a response to that which life speaks. A man's will is bound in the sense that he cannot decide whether to respond or not.

Luther uses the symbol *the word of God* to designate the soil and atmosphere in which life grows. This symbol, *the word, the word of life,* or *the word of God,* does not refer to any idea or concept with an exact and definable content. It stands for the fact that man's response to the speech of life is of central importance to the realization of humanness.

The word of life has a decisive bearing upon the formation of words. The word of God becomes Luther's basic symbol through the experiences described above, in which it becomes clear to him that the language of the church is in deep conflict with everyday language. He becomes aware that the doctrine and the proclamation of the church are a lifeless fabric of language spreading

its cover over the various areas of life, stifling the growth of a
web of living speech. The language used by parents, teachers,
rulers, and others who give shape to the verbal communication
in a community crushes the words growing like delicate plants
out of men's experiences of the vitalities of existence.

In his own being and growth Luther has experienced the threat
which the fragmentation of this vital language imposed upon his
whole existence as a human being. His study of the Bible has
revealed to him that this fragmentation is a threat not only to him
but to all human existence. Thus he conceives as a task of vital
importance the translation of the Bible into the language which
holds together the basic web of life in his community. Natural
language, he says, is the empress who is above all artificial tongues
(*über alle subtile, spitzige, sophistische dichtunge*, "above all sub-
tle, sharp, sophistic fiction").[63] In his work of translation he binds
together the language of the biblical writings and the language by
which his own community lives. The sacred writings preserve and
cultivate the sensitive vocabulary of the basic vitalities of human
existence. In his own society this vocabulary is being diminished
and mangled, especially by the language of the church. In trans-
lating the Bible he seeks a renewal of the language of his own
community, as he looks for "the germane and genuine word."

In becoming steeped in the sacred writings Luther feels such a
loosening of tongue and such an integration of words to new contexts as to thrill him to the depths of his being. Fountains burst
forth from which flow living waters to break down the fateful
watershed which had separated the stream of words into two
channels, the language of faith and the language of everyday life.
This "Pentecost experience," the experience of language made
whole, brings him to see in a new light the sacred writings which
had opened the fountains. He sees that these writings are themselves the result of the same kind of discovery of such springs of
life. He begins to see behind the writings the faces of the writers.
Through the Scriptures he is drawn into the company of living
men. He finds himself as a member of a large discussion circle,
extending through the centuries, in which men entangled in the
verbal meshes of various generations and communities have

learned to speak to one another in the basic language of life. The divine word of life integrates and holds together the being of man fragmented in his formation of words, as well as mankind splintered into various worlds of language. All human life is bound together by the divine word which molds the experiences of the ages into the history of mankind and structures men into one humanity.[64] Through interaction with the sacred writings Luther comes to the realization that only by the cultivation and transmission of the divine word of life do the separate elements of life grow together into a divine humanness, the reality which these writings describe as the people of God, the number of the elect, the household of God, the church and body of Christ. The sacred writings were given birth by the living word *(viva vox)*[65] which is the soil and atmosphere for all human life and growth.

Living communication between men, the language which creates humanity, implies a contact with the divine word *(deus per internum verbum immediate dicit*, "God speaks directly through the inner word").[66] Confrontation with the divine takes place in hearing and speaking the basic language of human existence. God himself speaks and hears in man *(qui in nobis loquatur et audiat*, "who speaks and hears in us").[67] Life's fundamental web is the kingdom of hearing.[68] Man lives by hearing *(natura verbi est audiri*, "the nature of the word is that it is heard").[69]

The word of life, the atmosphere of divine humanness, the air of trust which one must breathe to be a human being, cannot be dealt with as a reality separate from man. It cannot be defined by man. It gives birth to humanness and remains as much a mystery to man as the ultimate origin of his physical birth. The mystery is revealed in the men led by the spirit *(et ii vocantur dei formae homines et filii dei, qui spiritu dei aguntur*, "they are called men shaped by God and sons of God, who are led by the spirit").[70] The divine revelation grows forth as human communion. Men are to one another the means of divine revelation and grace, servants of the word of life.[71]

Luther claims that Erasmus denies the presence of this divine word in human life when he speaks of divine grace and the human world as two separate entities which must be brought together through the work and teaching of the church. To Erasmus the Scriptures and the church which is commissioned to transmit them are the specific means of grace. He regards as the basic decision of life the response of man to the grace which is offered by these means. Man is responsible for the reception of this grace. Man has the capacity to submit with God's help to guidance by grace or to spurn the divine offer of grace. Here is the freedom and the responsibility of human choice.

Luther replies that Erasmus's portrayal of the divine economy of grace reflects his thinking about life and reality in general.[72] According to Luther, a man cannot avoid describing reality in terms of his own experience. Knowledge of the divine cannot be detached from self-knowledge. What a man is determines what he thinks.

It is Luther's judgment that Erasmus elevates his own life-attitude, the approach of the scholar, to be the only divine one. He defends as scriptural a view of man in which to be a disciple of reality and to live in the subject-object relationship is the basic structure of human existence. He thus selects a specific area of life to be the ground for the divine-human encounter. He sets his own choice against divine election and his own word against the word of life.

The infuriated statements about the blindness of reason, contained in Luther's reply, are directed against the effort to posit as the starting point of the quest for encounter with the divine an approach which seeks to discern laws in reality.[73] To Luther this kind of thinking is only one form of thought. A view of man constructed on the foundation of the study of nature illumines only a narrow sector of human existence. One of Luther's basic aims is to show that this traditional view has come to dominate wrongly the totality of human existence. In this way misplaced reason tends to violate and destroy the fundamental threads of the web of life. Luther seeks to demonstrate that obedience to the word of life leads to a realization of humanness in diverse vocations and within various conceptions of human life.

In describing the relation between the divine and the human as an encounter between two factors, God's grace and man's will,

and in claiming that grace is the principal factor and man's will a
secondary one, Erasmus is in line with his portrayal of man as a
disciple of reality. According to this conception, nature with its
laws and principles has the most authority in human experience.
Man's lot is to make a choice between consent and refusal to be
taught by nature. Erasmus applies this line of reasoning to the
divine economy of grace. He emphasizes the decisive influence of
divine grace in man's salvation and says that the share of man's
will in it is quite insignificant. Even the freedom possessed by
the human will is the product of divine grace. Instructed and
redeemed by the divine will, man's will is able to make the right
choice. Luther says that Erasmus, like Aristotle, portrays God as
awaiting and observing men's decisions. He thus conceives God
as a being who once created the world but then left to man's will
the choice of his relationship to divine love and grace.

When one reads the Scriptures through the spectacles of this
view of God, most of its narratives and characters remain incomprehensible. The intertwining of the divine and the human manifest there remains hidden. Luther stresses that in the sacred writings, as in all life, there is a simultaneity of spirit and letter, gospel
and law, divine humanness and godless inhumanness, righteousness
and sin. The Scriptures speak of God as active in men, pardoning
and judging, loving and hating, electing and hardening, speaking
and listening. When the expression *God says* is used, it always
signifies that one man is speaking to another or to others about the
way in which the word of life has become clear in his experience.
The divine word reverberates in the hearts of Abraham, Isaac,
and Jacob, and of countless other human beings, giving birth to a
community of men which preserves and cultivates the language
of life.

According to Luther, Erasmus uses the Bible as though it were
divine revelation in the sense that a man living as a student of
reality discovers in it the divine law imbedded in life and the
divine plan of salvation which is to be realized through reality.
Luther contends that this use of the Bible is contrary to its true
content and spirit. When Erasmus, for example, appeals to the
authority of the apostles and says that their assertions prove man's

free will, Luther replies that only the divine word itself has genuine authority. It is wrong to assume that the apostles always express the truth because they are apostles and saints.[74] The conflict between spirit and flesh goes on also in them and in their writings. The sacred writings have not been preserved in order to transmit certain conceptions of God and of man. They bring us into the company of men contending for life, into that living interaction and communion in which the sacred writings were born.

If the Bible is used as an authority for proving the correctness of some concept of God or man, one must set the greater portion of the Bible aside, as Erasmus does. This is also the case if some specific divine revelation and plan of salvation is singled out in the Bible and then presented as the message of the Bible. After such a process the Scriptures are, as one scholar has said, like a squeezed lemon which can be thrown away once the juice has been extracted.

A basic thought in Luther's reply is that the word of God is not bound. The divine word and will is not a finished chapter.[75] Luther labels as atheists those who seek to improve life by supplanting the divine word and the divine humanness with ideals and programs of their own. When the divine word is tied to human regulations, its work of creating humanness is obstructed. Man lives in a cross fire. On the one side he is approached by the word of life which seeks to nurture him in divine humanness and to create unity with life and its Creator. On the other side he is attracted by forces which seek to draw him away from the divine word into efforts to build his life on some other foundation.

When Erasmus selects from the Scriptures examples to prove that man has a free will, Luther contends that not a single one of them points to human initiative in the creation of authentic humanness. All saints have prayed for life to be given to them. They have had the experience of trying to escape the divine word which is at work to make men give up positions contrary to life and to change the world of man. These men and their writings are called holy because they have become aware of the holiness of life and of the giver of life. The light of this holiness has exposed the unholiness, inhumanity, and idolatry residing in them and in their surroundings. They speak of the divine word of life, operative in all men and open to all, as a light shining in the darkness. They share with their fellowmen the experience of being ensnared again and again in webs of words which strangle the word of life. If this were not so, Luther says, all mankind could be changed by a single sermon of the word of life.

Holy men, however, are portrayed in the Scriptures as constantly cultivating the divine word. Among them a continuing discerning of spirits goes on. A fundamental task in their life is the differentiation between the spirit of life and the spirit of the flesh, divine humanness and godless inhumanness, holiness and unholiness.

In answering Erasmus's argument that a view may be proved right or wrong by means of the Bible, Luther points out that the writings of the Bible have been born out of the kind of experience which has led men to look for the boundary between the human and the inhuman and that they are thus involved in both.

Luther describes this involvement by speaking about two churches which have been opposed to each other from the beginning of the world. He calls them the church of Abel and the church of Cain.[76] Always and everywhere God's church confronts a wrong church, and divine humanness confronts an idolatrous inhumanness. Man becomes man and mankind becomes mankind through the process of differentiation between these realities. Men are either being integrated into a divine humanity, the church of God, or being fragmented into groupings which destroy the basic web of life, the wrong churches. The divine word and spirit create in men a texture of life which repairs the damage caused by the denial of life. This texture of grace, this kingdom, is not made by men.[77] It makes men. Humanness is received as a gift. It is born out of listening to the giver of life, out of being "hearers of God" (auditores dei).

Communion as the Soil in Which Life Grows

In speaking about the humanness which the word of life produces, Luther uses the word as the symbol of communion. Human life grows in the soil of communion. From this point of view it is impossible to speak about a will that is free from life's basic unifying connections. Luther therefore rejects Erasmus's conception of the fundamental orientation of human life, the positing of a separate human individual as a subject in confrontation with objective reality. Erasmus assumes that an individual has a will that is free and independent of the community of fellowmen, a capacity to conform or not to conform, in his own individual way, to what reality teaches. The divine will is thus assumed to confront man primarily as an ideal or an abstract command. Luther's emphasis, on the contrary, is that it confronts man as communal reality, embracing him as matrix of life.

When Luther accuses the church of exercising tyranny over men's lives, he does not refer merely to some specific abuses or to the harshness of some of its procedures. He charges that the main thrust of the work and teaching of the church breaks down the basic unities of life and severs the ties of mutual respect and confidence which bind men to one another.[78] He accuses both the spiritual and secular authorities of destroying the fundamental web of life. He reminds both of their obligation to protect the unities of life. If they do not do this, they suppress the word of God. In the basic "life-community" (*Gemeine, Gemeinschaft*) man encounters the giver of life (*Gott stehet in der Gemeine,* "God stands in the basic 'life-community' ").

Luther's conception of the divine texture of life becomes especially clear in his discussion of the church. The figure of the church of Abel and the church of Cain is worth bearing in mind. The story of mankind is the story of a conflict between a humanity obedient to the word of life and a humanity in opposition to it.

According to Luther, the word of life is the mother both of the Scriptures and of the churches. Just as the sacred writings preserve and transmit the communion which is experienced as the ground of life, so it is also preserved and transmitted by the structures and symbols designated as churchly. Churches carry on the search for contact with the basic texture of life, with the divine word which creates humanness, with the church of God (*sic constituitur ecclesia inter homines, quando fit cohabitatio dei cum hominibus,* "thus the church is constituted among men, when God lives in company with men").[79] The churches emerge out of the experience of the presence of the divine in human life (*nobiscum loquitur,* "he speaks with us").[80] Wherever the dialogue with life engenders obedience to the word of life, there the church of God is present (*ecclesiam esse per totam orbem terrarum,* "to be the church throughout the whole world").[81] The church of God is a treasure hidden in the field of human life (*ecclesia latet,* "the church is hidden").[82] The divine word vitalizes the basic "life-community," creating an interaction and mutuality in which, by cultivation of this word, one dwells in the basic web of life like branches on a vine (*tota vita et substantia ecclesiae est in verbo,* "the whole life and substance of the church is in the word").[83]

Luther recommends a change in the wording of the creed by substituting *Christian people (Christlich Volk)*[84] for *church,* because people, not the Bible or the church, are the basic "means of grace" of the divine word. The church of God grows out of people. God conceals his church in the midst of people. One can speak of the divine only as it is united with the human (*wo du mir Gott hinsetzest da mustu mir die menscheit mit hin setzen, sie lassen sich nicht sondern und von einander trennen,* "where you present God to me, there you must also present mankind to me, for they are not to be separated or torn apart from each other").[85]

Luther's emphasis on the presence of the divine as the ground of communion in human life is especially strong in his discussion of the person and work of Jesus. He criticizes the traditional *imitatio* piety which seeks to copy Jesus, for here Jesus is worshiped as a separate private person *(persona privata).*[86] He regards Erasmus's conception of "the philosophy of Christ,"[87] his instruction for humility in facing reality and divine revelation, as following this line.

What Luther here opposes is not only the effort to set up Jesus as an idol, as an absolute authority, in the same way in which the Bible, the church, the state, knowledge, or some other aspect of reality may be idolized. Luther sees something still more tragic about this view. To regard Jesus as the best student and teacher of reality is to conceal the divine word contained in his life, death, and resurrection, and the power of that divine word to create communion.

Luther speaks of Jesus as primarily the incarnation of the divine word of life, the emergence of divine humanness. He uses various expressions to warn against speaking about the divinity of Jesus in terms of the traditional authoritarian faith. For example, in his treatise on Christian liberty he charges the preachers of the church with presenting the words and deeds of Jesus in such a way as to elevate him to the isolated divinity of a private person, to be an object of faith and a divine authority for man. This kind of preaching generates a faith *(fides historica)* which has nothing to do with living in faith by the word of life. When the words and deeds of Jesus are proclaimed as this kind of divine revelation and the church calls men to this kind of obedience, Jesus is used for other purposes than the one for which he gave his life.

Jesus is the manifestation of life. His significance to other men does not consist in his being a divine revelation of some reality unknown to his fellowmen. The case is not that in him something previously unexpressed in words now takes the form of words but rather that what previously had been expressed in words now becomes flesh and life. The Scriptures portray the birth of the child of Bethlehem as the fulfillment of the promise that divine humanness is to be realized in spite of the enraged opposition of destructive powers fighting the incarnation of a true man.

The divinity of Jesus consists in his dedication to the service of the divine word, the word of life. The writings of the Bible are called sacred because they speak of men impelled into action by the divine word *(ob hanc causam haec historiae vocantur sacrae et communes sunt omnibus hominibus, habentibus verbum dei, in quibus deus operatur,* "for this reason these stories are called sacred and are common to all men who have the word of God and in whom God operates").[88] By means of the sacred writings Jesus enters into fellowship with such men of God. Their psalms become his prayers, their agonies and joys find their way into his heart, their life story becomes his life story. Thus he rises to gather up fragmented human being and the whole torn fabric of mankind into that texture of life which the divine word weaves. He experiences himself and he is experienced by others to be the "head" of an organism which thus comes into being, a body and a we-community integrated into the basic vitalities of existence. In the person and life of Jesus the whole organism of human existence is placed into new relationships.

The manifestation of life in Jesus is a burgeoning of humanness, revealing on the one hand the entanglement of mankind in a net which threatens to strangle life and to bring about a dehumanized humanity, and radiating on the other hand the word of life and the fundamental vitalities which must be recovered. With this in mind Luther can say that what the writers of the New Testament call the gospel is not itself the light but the unveiling of the true light, the light of life. In his reply to Erasmus, Luther uses the example of the temptation of Peter to regard himself as the representative of the world of light to the "pagan" Cornelius,[89] only to discover that Cornelius has already encountered the same light and the same spirit. Luther makes the same point in speaking about the encounter between Jesus and the Canaanite woman. Beneath the outward harshness of Jesus' dealing with the woman is the purpose to repel wrong worship of himself and to lead a mother, dejected because of self-accusation and rejection by others, to see the faith contained in her own heart.

Luther's writings yield numerous other examples of the way in which he sees Jesus awakening the people whom he confronts to experience the divine humanness, the texture of life, the kingdom of God, the faith, which is within themselves. It is from this point of view that Luther sees the acknowledgment of Jesus as the Christ, God's anointed, divine.

In the company of Jesus one experiences the reality of communion, of life in basic community. Jesus lives in his fellowmen and they in him in such a way that the word of life is released to heal the injuries resulting from the suppression and neglect of life's fundamental relations. His influence generates a mutuality of

human lives, a we-ness in which life about to become a dead web
of guilt is transformed into a living fabric of grace. In the growth
experienced here evil conscience becomes good conscience,
sickness becomes health, the bonds which shackle life become
new liberating connections.

Luther stresses in many contexts that Jesus and his church
cannot be separated from each other. Jesus is the Christ in being
what he is in his fellowmen and in their life in him. Just as to be
a mother, a father, or a child is to be in relationship to another,
not in relationship to oneself or to some norm of relationship, so
Jesus is the Christ through fellowship, through living in others
and for others.

Luther says that properly speaking only the Old Testament is
to be designated as Holy Scriptures. The content of the New
Testament is such that it cannot be put in writing. Jesus himself
thus writes nothing. Hence also those who experience in him and
in his company the manifestations of life, the construction of
communion, do not concentrate on preserving their experience
in literary form. Luther even goes so far as to say that he deplores the necessity of having the New Testament in men's hands
as a book. It deals with the kind of experience which writings are
quite inadequate to convey. It speaks of the experience of organic
unity shared by Jesus and his associates, of life in congregations
energized by the word of life. Such experience cannot be transmitted from one group to another or from one generation to another by means of writings or any other substitutes for the living
word (*viva vox, ein lebendig stym,* "living voice").[90] The Old
Testament too speaks of this kind of experience,[91] but within it
there is as yet no such activity of the word of life or such incorporation into the basic vitalities as in the experience of Jesus and
his associates. The Old Testament is Holy Writ *(Heylige schrift).*
The New Testament tells of a new kind of incarnation of the
word of life *(leyplich, lebendige wort; ecclesiam involutam esse
in carne;* "bodily, living word; church enveloped in flesh").[92]

When Luther speaks about the divine word as a living voice
(viva vox) and about the vocal *(vocali)* nature of its use, he does
not claim that the spoken word has more vitality than the written

word. Nor is the thrust of his criticism of the church's preaching
in any charge that the church has too little oral proclamation and
too much reading, nor in any charge that preachers are unfaithful
to the texts of the Bible. The point of his criticism is directed at
the basic structure of the church's office of preaching and teaching. He argues that the Bible has been written in an entirely
different spirit from the one in which it is being used in the
church.

Preaching is not oral transference of a given literary heritage
from one generation or group to another, nor is it transmission
of revelation from those to whom it has been given to those to
whom it is to be passed on. Preaching from the texts of the Bible
is organically related to that cultivation of the word of life, taking
place in countless different forms, which goes on in human
existence to deliver men from powers that suppress life. Every
man is a preacher and a priest in the sense that in his being the
word of life either becomes audible or is silenced. Every man is
a listener and responder to life. Human life is realized as a
dialogue in which every man is a word about life to his fellowman. Every fellowman is to be respected as one who listens and
responds to the speech of life. In the dialogue between men a
third participant, the divine word of life, is always present. Thus
human dialogue always has the nature of a trialogue.

This means that divine word and revelation cannot be encountered as a concept or idea separate from human beings. It
cannot be transferred from one generation or group to another
(*successio*) in the way in which an ideology is preserved. In the
cultivation of the divine word the sacred writings are not presented as a given revelation or ideology. The Holy Scriptures are
a book of life growing out of the word of life. It is transmitted
by men who together with the men of the Bible are exercised in
hearing and speaking the word of life. The Scriptures have been
born out of the unfolding of the word of life and its vital associations in the lives of men, and they lead into fellowship with men
living by this word and these associations.

In saying that the Bible "drives" to Christ or "chases" Christ
(*Christum agere*), Luther is not speaking about a view or concept

of Christ but about the living Christ present in men's lives (*in ipsa fide Christus adest*, "in faith itself Christ is present").[93] He has this in mind when he says that in seeking contact with Jesus one must find his church. He does not mean that churches are the representatives of divine reality in the world but that the divine word is contained in the dialogue with life carried on in these human communities. Likewise, in saying that outside the churches there is no truth and no Christ, he means that truth does not confront a man as an abstract idea but as an incorporation into life's basic associations and a discovery of vital communion. The divine is encountered in human community, and the divine word is encountered as incarnate in humanity (*ego nullo de deo scio quam in hac humanitate*, "I know nothing about God other than what is in this humanity").[94]

The divinity of Jesus is precisely in his complete humanness. Luther also says that the humanness of Jesus is not merely in his historical and physical being but in the whole structure of life produced by his spirit. Luther is thus enabled to declare every man to be a Christ to his fellowman.

In the interpretations of Luther his strong emphasis on the proclamation of the word and the administration of the sacraments has often been detached from the contexts in which he speaks of them.[95] In the Lutheran tradition the phrase *the word and the sacraments* has often become a misleading slogan. This is the case especially when the word and the sacraments are regarded as the only proper means of grace. Such thinking leads to that very conception of the function of the church which Luther questioned.[96]

In his reply to Erasmus Luther not only seeks to show that Erasmus's use of the Bible is contrary to the divine word, but he also makes the same criticism of his view of the authority of the church. According to Luther, Erasmus regards his own church as God's chosen vehicle for transmitting divine revelation to men. It is Luther's argument, as we have already observed, that the true church of God, the living organism created by the word of life, is actually imprisoned by the church. If some ecclesiastical structure sets itself up as the channel and mediator of divine revelation and grace, classifying some men as mediators of grace and others as its receivers, it is opposed to the divine word which uses every man as its "means of grace." Erasmus thus has the wrong kind of obedience to the church. His theology rationalizes the significance of a specific ecclesiastical organization.

When Protestants use the expression *the word and the sacraments* as their slogan, they are actually defending the kind of organization of church life in which men are divided, in accordance with the medieval pattern,[97] into mediators and receivers of grace, proclaimers and hearers of divine revelation, participants in divine reality through the Scriptures and nonparticipants lacking in knowledge of the Scriptures. In this way the doctrine of the word and the sacraments becomes an ideology for rationalizing a form of church activity. It is this kind of church-centered structuring of a theology of revelation that Luther attacks in speaking of human beings as the primary channels and mediators of divine grace.

Luther does not replace the proclamation of the word and the administration of the sacraments in the church with some other ecclesiastical system as "means of grace." His main emphasis in speaking to his own church is that the proclamation of the word and the administration of the sacraments must be done in the spirit of the gospel in order to fulfill vital functions which have been neglected.

Luther's speech concerning the word and the sacraments takes on a somewhat different emphasis in his discussions with the "fanatical" theologians *(Schwärmer)*.[98] Appealing to Luther, the fanatical movements often tended to seek the destruction of common public worship with its preaching from biblical texts and its use of the sacraments. In these movements Luther detects the same kind of utopian ideology and rationalism as in the revolutionary social movements of his time. He sees in this utopianism a lack of reverence for the basic structure of life. Both the divine and the human are treated as ideological realities separate from the fundamental associations of life and useful for shaping life as one pleases. In such contexts Luther speaks his sharpest words about the inability of human reason to understand life and the encounter with the divine. When man is detached from life's actual basic associations he imagines himself to be the creator of his own life and environment, and he becomes violent in his relation to life and to his fellowmen. A utopian rationalist is cruel both toward reality and to his fellowmen, for he demands that everything be changed in accordance with his own reason and his own view of reality.

The church and the fanatical movements, Luther says, are actually like two foxes with their tails tied together, for both seek to govern reality and men with the authority of some specific vision. To the fanatics Luther points out that in despising the writings of the Bible and the sacraments they are despising life itself. To cherish the Scriptures and the sacraments is to take care of the roots of life and the living word. The Scriptures incorporate men into the multifibered living fabric of mankind by uniting them with men living by the word of life. Baptism and the Lord's Supper likewise bind men to the underlying nexus of life, the living communion which cannot be expressed by any ideas or concepts. Reverent use of them maintains a connection with the radiant glow beneath the surface of life, the love that dissolves the walls separating men from one another and from the giver of life. Whether he is addressing the church or the fanatics, Luther's emphasis is the same: life must be revered, not tyrannized.

Luther's thinking is governed by the perspective of communion. He asks, what kind of "fellowmanhood" is genuine communion, what is the nature of the nexus of life's basic connections, how is the fabric of life put together? He sees the divine will and revelation confronting man as communion, not as abstract laws and principles. With a variety of images and ideas he describes this fundamental structure of all human life. He uses images drawn from the sphere of family and home, pointing out that the church of God grows out of the human family. The strands of the texture of life are traceable where father, mother, and child are in intercommunion. At times he pictures this basic structure as a network of various callings in life.[99] Here the ties which hold the community of life together are men's interrelations as they fulfill their different vocations. Luther also portrays the underlying unity as an intercellular matrix which contains all men from the first generation to the last.[100] Here the threads of the fabric of life are seen as binding the generations to one another, linking together the past, the present, and the future. In whatever perspective Luther examines the communionlike nature of life, his essential emphasis is that human life is not rooted in impersonal laws and ideas but in the living unities[101] realized in reciprocal giving and receiving.

Faith as the Basic Situation of Life

Most often Luther portrays *communio*, the underlying community of life, as a texture of faith and love.[102] The divine confronts man as a *communio* in which the word of life is in twofold action. On the one hand it creates faith, through which it maintains connections with the ground and giver of life. On the other hand the same word binds men to one another, creating an interrelationship of love, of giving and receiving, of living in and for one another.

In saying that man is justified through faith and not through the performance of good deeds, Luther does not mean by faith some orientation to reality which is to replace good deeds as a way to a confrontation with the divine. He does not speak of faith as either an act of merit or an act of acknowledging the lack of merit, as any act by which man achieves contact with the divine. Faith means to Luther above all that basic human situation in which man, such as he is, is addressed by the word of life. In his reply to Erasmus, Luther describes this situation as bondage of the will. The situation of faith is man's fundamental orientation to life. To live as a human being is to live by faith.

Becoming a man does not begin with what a man makes of himself. The basic situation of being human is not the kind of discipleship of reality in which man decides what he is to become by the attitudes which he assumes. Man does not create his own being. He does not grow into humanness by his own knowledge of good and evil and by the deeds which he performs on this basis. Man is not justified by his knowledge and action (*non ex opere per scientiam*, "not from action through knowledge").

In describing the basic human situation as faith, Luther emphasizes that the very fact of being human is man's first reality. Man is not primarily a disciple of reality but a plot of soil[103] in which the seed of humanness is planted (*ad primam gratiam . . . nos habemus passive sicut mulier ad conceptum*, "toward primary grace we are as passive as a woman toward conception").[104] Becoming a human being takes place in a situation in which a man, so to speak, gives birth to his own humanness. This basic situation summons man to grow into a person (*fides facit personam*, "faith makes a person"). He is to become not a mere observer of reality but a working companion of the Creator, sharing with him the creation of life. Such humanness is the realization of the divine plan of creation: "Let us make man."

Faith is an act of God, not a human achievement. Just as nature impels the animals to act according to their instincts, so the word of life which creates humanness operates in faith to impel a man to grow into a man. The starting point of becoming human is not an attitude which man assumes toward reality. It is the word of life. Being a man is not something that is attained. It is received as a gift. This is the most important emphasis in Luther's constantly repeated statements that a man does not become good by doing good deeds, that he does not become righteous by acting righteously, that by being good he does good and by being righteous he performs acts of righteousness.

In repudiating Erasmus's conception of humanness as a situation in which man is in a position to decide between the alternatives confronting him, Luther does not set up some other view of man. His central aim is to show that humanness cannot be defined from any point of view outside the divine-human encounter, the word of life and the response to it. Luther does not define in a new way the traditional conception of the prerequisites for encountering the divine and of the surest way of finding the divine.

Luther's conception of the central task of his theology is to clear the way for listening to the word of life. He repudiates all efforts to define man, saying that the acts of God provide this

definition. Man is not to define himself but to submit to being
defined by the word of life. When some area of experience is
conceived to be the starting point and presupposition for encountering the divine, when some form of humanness is defined as
divine, then the door is closed to the word of life. This is unfaith,
the direct opposite of faith which alone enables man to realize
humanness in obedience to the word of life. To become man is
a matter of creation. Humanness is not born automatically but is
the result of divine creative activity (*creaturae procedunt ex deo
libere et voluntarie et non naturaliter*, "creatures come forth from
God freely and voluntarily, not naturally").

Being human is not passive study of what life is about but
active participation in creation. To be a listener to the word of
life implies obedience to life. This is what Luther has in mind
in saying that faith leads man into a life which is outside human
experience (*extra nos*, "outside ourselves").[105] Men obedient to
the word of life are divine acts of creation (*facta dei*), and their
growth into humanness does not depend upon themselves but
upon the creative activity of the divine word (*extra se; in deo
eligente salutem suam consistere*, "outside oneself; to depend for
one's welfare upon divine election"). Life wells up in faith.
Divine humanness is realized in a continuing dialogue with life
which brings constant deliverance from "dead works" into
creative action (*semper incipere*, "always to begin"). When
Luther speaks of men of faith as passive (*sancti sunt passiva*,
"saints are passive"), he refers to openness to the speech of life
and its rich content, to liberation to receive life in its manifold
splendor.

Luther regards Erasmus's view as a withdrawal from the word
of life, an escape from openness to the vitalities of existence. He
considers Erasmus's concept of man to be mechanistic. In
portraying man as a nursling of reality, as a free will, Erasmus
conceives of man as a being whose primary function is to react
to the stimuli which reality provides.[106] In presenting the grounds
for his thesis of free will, Erasmus says that unless man has the
ability to achieve something, there is no room for merits, and
unless there is room for merits, punishments and rewards lose

their significance. For this reason, Erasmus continues, man cannot be mere "flesh." He must have soul and spirit, the capacity to react to the alternatives of existence and to the punishments and rewards thus implied, the capacity to strive for what is best for him. Reason must operate in him to control the instincts.

It is precisely upon this contention that Luther concentrates his criticism of Erasmus's view of man. When Erasmus describes man as a bodily being, directed by soul and reason, he leads him into detachment from life's basic associations, to a fragmentation of his true being, to a dangerous floating above life. Luther regards as dangerous this separation of body and soul, experience and thought. To Luther thought and soul are a dimension of man's basic existence, which is bodily existence. Thoughts and words serve to bind men to one another and thus to form a nexus of life in which they live in interaction and interdependence. A man's words and thoughts are thus not primarily his own, for in them life speaks to him,[107] and through them he lives in his fellowmen and they in him. Nor is a man's body a separate area of existence but an organic part of the nexus of life in which men together constitute the body of humanity. Whether man is viewed in his psychic or bodily dimensions, as reason or as experience, he is fundamentally a being who lives in associations and creates associations, not a puppet of external reality.

Luther labels as ridiculous the attempt to speak of a divine-human encounter in mechanistic terms. What Erasmus says about free will concerns some mechanisms of human behavior which have their own place and function in human life. Luther declares that when the discussion concerns this level of thought he has no objection to what Erasmus says about free will. He does not deny the abundance and significance of mechanical behavior in human life, of attitudes determined by specific conditions. He speaks in numerous contexts, as noted above, about the significance of the "works of the law" for the construction and preservation of the communal life (the first use of the law). He also regards the appeal to rewards and punishments and the acknowledgment of "merit" as having an important function in education. To Luther, the tragedy of Erasmus's view is in the fact that he applies this form of human behavior to the whole reality of human experience, although it is actually only a surface phenomenon. Thus he denies that the divine word, the word of life, is present in human reality.

In criticizing the church's effort to train its members into obedience to the divine will by means of temporal and eternal punishments and rewards, Luther is not blind to the fact that this system is in many respects quite efficient. In fact he admits its power to be so strong that it tends to suppress men's conscience. Man has a strong attraction for the kind of mechanical life in which he can live without scruples under the control of various external powers. Erasmus is right in saying that man's actual conduct obeys the norms which he has projected and that such mechanisms have an extensive foothold in the life of society. It is totally incomprehensible to Luther, however, how Erasmus can regard this will, determined by the objective world and merely reacting to it, as a free will and characteristic of the divine in man. Nor does Luther deny the rationality emphasized by Erasmus. He recognizes conformity to objective realities as belonging to the nature of thinking. Reason may indeed be considered as that form of human life in which man seeks to discover the universally valid laws of reality and to conform his thinking to them. Such activity has an important function in the shaping of human life. While Luther does not deny this, it is again incomprehensible to him how Erasmus can regard this activity as the most important one in facing life. From Luther's standpoint such a view is blind idolatry of human thinking.

Luther's statements on the bound will have often been conceived as material for constructing a new view of man to take the place of Erasmus's view. Such an interpretation yields highly questionable conclusions. For example, Luther is said to have supplanted the emphasis on the central importance of human reason with the view that the will is the decisive factor in human conduct. He is alleged to have rejected intellectualism in favor of voluntarism, claiming that knowledge does not direct man's will but is only its instrument. His insistence on the bound will is thus conceived as an antiidealistic protest against the idealistic view of man. His arguments concerning the bound will would thus serve the purpose of demonstrating the total depravity of the human will, of stressing that with his own capabilities and actions man cannot establish contact with the divine. According to this interpretation, Luther would have sought to show the idealist Erasmus that there is nothing good in man.

Divine Thinking and the Idolatry of Thinking

The main purpose of the foregoing analysis has been to set forth the thesis that the basic aim of Luther's reply is to repudiate the way in which Erasmus speaks of God and man. In setting himself in opposition to the traditional concepts of God and of man he does not seek to replace them with new views representing his own theology. He questions the validity of speaking about an encounter with God when the starting point is any concept of God or of man. He does not simply oppose the effort to find in the Bible an image of man with which one must comply (imitatio) in order to discover the way to the fulfillment of the divine will. His basic point of view is that one must give up the effort to select from the world of experience any starting point or foundation upon which to construct life.

It is life that elects man, not man that elects life. Growth into humanness takes place in a continuing dialogue with life. Man is primarily a being to whom life speaks and whom life calls to share in creation. Only in a secondary sense is man a being who speaks about life. To Luther the proper task of theology is to clear the way for the word of life and to demolish those structures of thought and life which obstruct the communication of the word of life. In saying that the basic task of theology is to distinguish between the law and the gospel, he has in mind the task of mediating the word of life. The purpose of this distinction is to keep the divine word free from entanglement with any structure of thought or form of life.

Luther sees such structures of thought in the traditional theology founded upon idealistic views. He does not deny the significance of idealistic thinking which seeks to analyze universal abstractions and to create norms to regulate nature and human life. The divine and the human may indeed be discussed in categories which man creates when as subject he investigates the world of objects, categories which he derives from the world of nature. Such discussion constitutes an important contribution toward the clarification of the content of the speech of life. But when all discourse concerning the divine and the human is forced into the categories and alternatives of this type of discussion, then the dialogue with life itself is disrupted. Luther views the thinking of Erasmus as leading to this result and therefore attempts to create discussion in new dimensions.

Luther does not replace idealistic with antiidealistic thinking, or human reason with some specific divine revelation. He does not set up a form of thinking based on revelation to be the guiding principle of discussion. This would mean only a replacement of one thought with another. The thrust of Luther's criticism is that Erasmus separates thinking from the rest of human experience and that he gives thinking an unwarranted place in relation to the total experience of life. Luther argues that Erasmus here follows blindly the views of the idealistic—particularly the Aristotelian—tradition.

In criticizing Erasmus for allowing Aristotle to govern his thinking, Luther is not speaking about the great ancient philosopher as a natural scientist. In this respect Luther himself regards Aristotle as an authority. The point of his criticism is directed at Aristotle as theologian. Here Luther focuses attention upon an aspect of thought which is today in the foreground of the study of ancient philosophy.[108]

Contemporary analysis of the theological structure of the idealism and humanism founded upon the tradition of antiquity has made clear that Plato and Aristotle lived in a time dominated by religion and mythology. It was a time in which life was experienced as a reality transcending human capacities. In such a situation they sought to distinguish the true rational core of religion from its mythical elements. They set forth from the world of nature the divine principles which support and guide all reality. They approached the God *(Theos)* who is the object of religious worship by analyzing the rationality *(Logos)* inherent in reality. Out of this effort grows theology, a study which has obtained a strong foothold in Western tradition, an attempt to analyze the divine basis of reality.

The word *theology* sees the light of day for the first time in the writings in which Plato presents the theological structure of his ideal state. Plato's fundamental purpose is to create a philosophical theology which defines the nature of divine reality. Aristotle likewise gives the name *theology* to the most important portion of his philosophy, for it deals with reality which transcends the physical world. Plato and Aristotle construct a rational theological approach to supernatural transcendent reality. They represent a theological humanism which seeks to prove the divine nature of human life and to show mortal man the way to participation in eternal life. When the views of the founders of idealism are understood this way, their thinking may be described as God-centered, for they examine the content of all human life and all reality by holding the divine to be the absolute norm of perfection and the basic principle of all existence.

The present study is limited to an examination of Luther's reaction to this tradition of theological humanism which he sees represented by Erasmus. Luther repudiates this kind of God-centered thinking. Basic to his appraisal is the contention that this view does not lead to thinking about the divine but makes thinking itself divine. Underneath this view he detects the attitude of regarding as the most certain and reliable experience of life that which man through his thinking has come to accept as universally valid and objective (*universalia sunt realia*, "universals are realities").[109]

Reference has already been made to the type of explanation which traces the roots of Luther's criticism of this view to nominalistic thought, according to which universal ideas are only names given to reality, while the most reliable experience comes from the contact with reality afforded by the will and emotion. Reason does not determine men's attitudes; it is experience that directs reason. According to nominalism, the divine does not confront man primarily as concepts and ideas but as the kind of reality which man cannot grasp with his reason and thought. In confronting the divine, man must refrain from using the standards by which he decides what is universally valid and objective, and submit to direct encounter with the divine. To nominalism experience of the divine is radically subjective.

The fact is that the thrust of Luther's antiidealistic critique is entirely different from that of nominalism. Unlike the nominalists, he does not stay within the area of the questions raised by idealism. Nominalism does not question the basic starting point of idealism. It is essentially antiidealism. It proceeds, however, from the same starting point as idealism, for it too considers the state of being educated by reality as the fundamental situation of human life. It differs from idealism in its conception of what is most reliable and certain experience, but it has the same conception of man as primarily a being who is fashioned by reality. Luther's criticism is focused precisely on this point. The basic situation of being human cannot be defined in terms of subject-object. The associations which it involves require entirely different categories.

Luther seeks to formulate these categories of association, as noted above, chiefly in terms of faith-love. It is in these terms that he describes the essential condition of being human. If the subject-object formulation is regarded as the basic situation of life, then faith is an external objective power holding sway over man, and love consists in acts through which the purposes of objective reality are realized in man. When Luther criticizes this traditional way of understanding the meaning of faith and love, he does not follow nominalism in stressing the significance of subjective experience as over against an overestimate of objectivity. Nor does he defend emotional and volitional experience against the attitude of ascribing undue importance to reason. When he speaks of faith and love as the fundamental situation of humanness, he is seeking an escape from the traditional formulation for conceiving the relation between the divine and the human.

While Luther considers the attempt to dominate life as inherent in human thinking and therefore portrays reason as resisting confrontation with the divine, he does not present the divine-human encounter as an irrational or suprarational event. He speaks about the inclination of human reason and thought toward idolatry, its effort to construct out of the fragments of reality which it has perceived to be objective a god ruling over all reality. He can thus say that men are manufacturers of gods *(fabricatores deorum)*. But he does not belittle the attempt of reason to grasp what is universally valid and objective.

In his reply to Erasmus, Luther often underscores the idea that "natural" reason actually understands the encounter with the divine as taking place within the limitations of a bound will. But man is unable to think such an idea through or to cling to it amid the crosscurrents of life. In one passage of his reply he speaks of the unbearable distress which this thought has caused him and of his constant attempts to get rid of it. The idea itself is not at all difficult to grasp. Even a little child can understand it. Man does not evade it because it is contrary to reason or transcends reason. Man seeks to escape such a thought because he seeks to escape life. But man becomes free to live only by thinking about life as it actually is. In refusing to think, man flees from the fundamental situation of life—from faith.[110] To escape faith man must cease to think.

In one respect Luther follows the same line as the idealistic tradition which he criticizes. He too holds the essence of thinking to be the effort to obtain contact with objective reality. But his view differs from that of idealism as regards the way in which thinking is anchored in the human person and his experience. He regards thinking as welling up from man's innermost depths in the same way as the rest of man's being and acting. In his thinking man is not outside the struggle of existence but shares in it. But even in his thinking man is tempted to shut himself off from life and to justify himself by that very thinking. When idealistic thinking becomes idealistic fancy, substituting its ideas for the word of life, it becomes the enemy of life. While thinking emerges from life, it turns against life when it seeks to absolutize itself.[111] Such an orientation to life[112] leads to a partition of human experience, a splitting into the separate areas of body and soul, sense experience and thought.

Humanness as Growth[113]

Luther claims that the traditional views on education, prevalent both in church and society, are in conflict with the basic situation of life. He says that the schooling and training which he received robbed him of his childhood. His language is most tender when he speaks about his children and writes to them or when he sings and preaches about the child Jesus.[114] The image of the child also assumes central importance in his theological vocabulary. The figures of teacher and pupil, one who nurtures and one who is nurtured, do not dominate his world of thought. In his writings one sees the faces of mother, father, and child.

This aspect of Luther's thought may reflect to some degree a romantic idealization of the child, understandable in a monk who had made the transition from a monastery to life in a family, or the revolt of a man of strong emotions against the over-intellectualized and harsh training which he had received. But it also expresses Luther's view of the nature of the encounter between the divine and the human. A theologian who studies this encounter, Luther says, must begin where God begins his work of making man, the mother's womb (*incipe ubi incipit, ab utero matris*, "begin where he begins, the mother's womb"). With various figures of speech Luther sets forth his emphasis that theology goes astray if it proceeds from the top of the tree rather than its roots, if it is concerned with some other reality than the divine humanness, the *communio* created by the word of life to be the basic community of life.

One of the fundamental concepts in the thought of Erasmus is learning *(eruditio)*.[115] Like Aristotle and Thomas Aquinas, he proceeds from the assumption that every man has an inborn desire for knowledge. Inherent in the being of man is the potential for growth through learning. When this potential is actualized in the right way, man grows in the direction of fulfillment. God has created the desire for knowledge in man, and the learning of true knowledge leads to him. The axiomatic starting point of Erasmus's view of man is the idealistic conception of nature as a rational reality.

Although the tradition of idealistic thought contains two sharply different views of the relation between man and nature, the Platonic and the Aristotelian, it is characteristic of all idealism founded upon the heritage of antiquity to speak of the nature of man and to view man from the standpoint of nature. According to the Platonic view, man confronts nature as something outside himself, as an objective world which transcends the subject. Here man is instructed by natural reality and is thus led to self-sacrifice and commitment to supernatural reality. According to the Aristotelian view, the natural is contained in man's own being as a potentiality which is actualized in the confrontation with the objective world. Here the emphasis is that by being a student of reality man is led to realize the possibilities within himself. The Augustinian theological tradition follows primarily the Platonic line of thought, while the Thomistic tradition is Aristotelian.[116]

The controversy between Erasmus and Luther has often been regarded as an echo of the clash between the Aristotelian-Thomistic and the Platonic-Augustinian views. Luther with his Augustinian heritage has thus been regarded as a theologian who stresses divine transcendence, setting his God-centered view against the man-centered view of Erasmus. Luther would then represent the theocentrism of the Christian tradition, and Erasmus the humanism based on the heritage of antiquity.

This is not the issue, however, with which Luther deals when he sets his dialectic of law-gospel against the scholastic synthesis of nature-grace.[117] He admits that the insights contained in the traditional syntheses have worth in the attempt to understand the structure of reality. Luther's thinking is quite similar in many respects to the Aristotelian philosophy of nature represented by Thomas Aquinas. Luther does not disregard the fact that scholastic theology makes a profound effort to show the organic inter-relatedness of grace and nature as well as of the divine and the human. Grace does not destroy nature but perfects it *(gratia non tollit sed perficit naturam)*. Luther too seeks to overcome the dichotomy which both classical and Christian traditions have brought into Western thinking, the division which Thomas sought to escape by creating a synthesis of twofold truth *(duplex veritas)*, the rational and the revealed. But Luther does not create a new synthesis of grace and nature, the divine and the human, faith and reason. With his dialectic of law and gospel he offers the tradition of dichotomy new dimensions of exploration for wholeness.

One of the chief aims of the idealistic tradition is to discover harmony between the various elements of life. It seeks to build a system of education by means of which balance and harmony may be established between the rational and the irrational elements of human existence, between the body and the soul. The same basic aim is evident in the striving of scholastic theology for a synthesis of reason and faith.

The tradition of theological idealism from which Luther emerges is marked by a tension between two views on the relation between faith and reason. The main trend is the attempt to show that Christan faith teaches the right way of thinking *(credo ut intelligam,* "I believe in order to understand"). But this striving for a synthesis between faith and reason also encounters severe criticism, and many theologians try to show that it is dangerous from the Christian point of view. They contend that the unique greatness of the Christian faith lies in the fact that it is not bound to any system of thought. To these systems Christianity appears in fact to be irrational and contradictory in many respects *(credo quia absurdum,* "I believe because it is absurd").

The theologians emphasizing the irrational or suprarational nature of faith claim that Christian intuition affords much more reliable knowledge of divine reality than does rational thought. Those who obey the eternal divine revelation disregard human opinions. From this point of view Luther appears as a theologian who rises from the stream of idealism to issue an antiidealistic protest, to defend faith against reason. He is therefore described as a fideist, one who attacks intellectualism and rationalism on the basis of some religious experience or doctrine. In extreme cases this type of interpretation has given Luther the label of a barbaric antihumanist who sets a paradoxical Christianity in opposition to the cultural ideals of classical antiquity.

Obviously Luther's reply to Erasmus did call for a reexamination of some basic cultural and educational principles which had been regarded as self-evident. The various traditional systems of education were all based on the view represented by Erasmus's concept of man as a student of reality. This became particularly clear in the structure of the universities,[118] the most important centers of the world of education. Both the teaching and the research in them were based on two principles, authority and reason. The authority is some objective reality—the historical, the natural, or the supernatural world. This objective reality is man's teacher. The task of reason is to analyze it and to transfer to the new generation the essentials of what it says. The goal of education is to liberate a man from his own individual opinions and feelings, based only on his own experience, and to lead him to share the riches of both natural and supernatural reality. Various methods are used in striving for this goal, but all agree that the human quest is primarily a process of learning. Virtue can be taught, and knowledge is the basic virtue.

From the standpoint of the issue explored in the present study, the particular significance of Luther's reply to Erasmus lies in the fact that it focused attention in a radical way on the essential nature of the views on which the educational systems of Western culture were based, the views on how humanness is to be realized.

Werner Jaeger, one of the most prominent investigators of the heritage of antiquity, writing on the relations between humanism and theology, presents Erasmus as a pioneer of humanism.[119] He declares that Erasmus's book *Enchiridion Militis Christiani* is a humanist manifesto. Jaeger regards Erasmus's humanism, presented as the philosophy of Christ, as a new form of Christian theology in which the emphasis is on education rather than dogmas. Erasmus is a theological humanist who purges the scholastic tradition of its antihumanistic elements.

In portraying the difference between Greek philosophers and Christian theologians, Jaeger describes the Christian view as a theology based on revelation. Christian theology is characterized by the quest for a synthesis between revealed suprarational theology and rational natural theology, between the Bible and the thinking grounded on the heritage of antiquity.

In his analysis of the humanistic elements in the theology of Thomas Aquinas, Jaeger describes Thomas as the outstanding medieval representative of the Greek ideal of man, one who cleared the way for the concept of human nobility advocated by the Renaissance humanists. Like the ancient humanists, particularly Aristotle, Thomas considers as most important for the achievement of humanness the capacity of man to act and to conduct himself (*agere et facere*, "to act and to do") in such a way as to be able to learn from reality. According to the Greek ideal of humanness and education (*paideia*), Jaeger says, man's strongest instinct, the basis of all education and progress, is the instinct of imitation. Man's nobility consists in his being a learner. Referring to Cicero's description of the humanizing influence of the Greek period, Jaeger traces this influence to the fact that in the life of the Greeks the ideal of humanness was set up with unique clarity for men to see. Other nations created gods, kings, and spiritual beings; the Greeks created men.

From the standpoint of the theme of the present study it is not important to discuss what interpretation of Erasmus or of Luther is best in doing justice to the historical data. By referring to various interpretations we are seeking to set forth the data, often overlooked by interpreters, which have the most importance for the discussion of our specific theme. Jaeger's analysis of the relation between humanism and theology is important in giving expression to an approach widely accepted in current research.

When Luther's reply to Erasmus is examined in the light of Jaeger's approach, it exhibits an outburst of rage against humanism. Obviously this is also the way in which Erasmus understood it. He says that Luther relies very little upon education and mostly upon the Holy Spirit. Thus also, in many studies analyzing the views of Erasmus, Luther is described as an arbitrary religious subjectivist. Erasmus opposes Luther, for he sees Luther's influence leading to a decay of education and the world of learning. Erasmus regards Luther as a revolutionary reformer who is obstructing with his dogmatism the success of the renewal which he claims to be bringing about. According to these interpretations, Luther in his reply to Erasmus makes erroneous and irresponsible statements which undercut all morality and result in doubting and underestimating the possibilities of education.

This approach is evident also in interpretations which portray Erasmus as a man who studied the Bible and dealt with theological problems according to the critical methods of humanism,[120] while Luther allegedly held such a procedure to be impossible. The contention is that Erasmus's study of the Bible is marked by respect for scientific accuracy and scholarship, while Luther's use of the Bible is characterized as arbitrary. When Luther repudiates the setting up of the Bible as an objective reality toward which one is to assume the attitude of a disciple, he is accused of being an enemy of scholarship. According to interpretations of this type, Luther gained a wider sphere of influence than Erasmus because the people of that day sought faith and were not yet mature enough to accept the objective critical position represented by Erasmus.

Luther is thus considered to be a theologian of revelation who seeks to prove the incapacity of human reason and will to deal with the matters of which divine revelation speaks. When Luther argues in his reply for the clarity of the Bible, he is understood to mean that the Bible is clear and bright in matters of faith. The true purpose of Luther's reply is construed to be the separation of faith and reason, by which faith rules in the realm of revelation, and reason in the world of human experience.

When Luther is understood in this way, he turns out to be on the one hand a dogmatic theologian of revelation and on the other hand a pioneer of "sound reason." The task of theology would thus be the study of the realm of revelation and suprarational reality, while the area of reason would be man's experience in nature and society. Theology should not meddle with matters outside its own field, with questions in which reason is the arbiter, nor should reason attempt to inquire and speculate about matters which transcend human understanding.

Luther's theology is thus viewed as leading on the one hand to a dogmatism in the interpretation of revelation and on the other hand to an agnostic attitude toward all metaphysical philosophizing. Luther has a spirit of subjective certainty on matters of faith pertaining to transcendent reality, but he is a critical rationalist in his relation to this-worldly reality.

We have already pointed out, however, that to Luther this kind of synthesis between revelation and reason is an untenable compromise. According to Luther, Erasmus combines a submission to divine authority and a skeptical attitude toward human experience in a way which fragments man's being and conscience. The thrust of Luther's criticism is against the position which causes one to speak of the divine in a spirit of absolutism and of the human in a spirit of relativism.

Luther seeks in his reply to point out the universal human proportions and dimensions of the issue under discussion. To him the issue does not concern various interpretations of tradition, although Erasmus attempts to conduct the debate on this level. The crucial problem for Luther is not the relationship between revelation and reason, the Bible and classical antiquity, theological and humanistic tradition. He does not place "pure" biblical Christianity in opposition to the classical tradition, nor does he propose a new synthesis between them. Luther examines both the theological and the philosophical elements of tradition from the same point of view, evaluating both in terms of whether the communication of the word of life is facilitated or hindered.

Johann Huizinga, in his study of Erasmus and the age of the Reformation,[121] deals with the controversy between Erasmus and Luther by noting that Erasmus remains an observer of the events taking place and deplores the tragedy of the commotion, while Luther deliberately enters into the whirl of events. Erasmus's use of words is serenely objective, while Luther's is wildly ecstatic, the language of a man trying to say something that cannot be expressed in words. Huizinga's description sets forth an important insight.

Erasmus emphasizes again and again that the goal of thinking is accord and harmony. Nothing is more distasteful to him than the incitement of discord between men. The tone and style of Luther's reply is completely different from that of Erasmus and of the scholastic tradition. Luther's thinking does not evade the contradictory, the disordered, the incomprehensible. He admits into his world of thought wars, massacres, rebellions, whatever the historical situation offers as material for thought. Luther responds in his writings to questions awakened in his mind by the events of his own time. He thinks aloud in public without fear of causing discord. His writing has a conversational character. Both the strength and weakness of Luther's reply to Erasmus become manifest in his boisterous and often violent use of language.

Luther's language, unbridled and careless from the standpoint of both theological and philosophical tradition, has often been regarded as simply the expression of his temperament. But it can also be examined in the light of the fact that Luther's thoughts run counter to the traditional ways of thinking. Luther has to express his ideas in the same kind of situation in which an exponent of a new scientific theory finds himself in conversing with representatives of views which he repudiates. In such a situation the new language appears quite arbitrary from the point of view of the old. Especially in a situation in which a "scientific faith" or a "revealed knowledge"[122] is completely predominant, a pioneer of research has to resort to wild-sounding language in order to gain a hearing.

Luther's reply contains power that breaks down thought forms which are imbedded in the established alternatives. This is particularly evident when he points out how remotely connected with the vitalities of existence a man remains when he is content to be only a disciple and observer of reality and to evade creative suffering. The weakness of the reply lies in Luther's abortive effort to express in words and concepts a reality which defies verbalization and conceptualization. Thus Luther is often led to present the kind of "theology of glory" *(theologia gloriae)* in which one speaks of reality as if man could examine it from a divine point of view, the "theology of glory" which he himself opposes with his "theology of the cross" *(theologia crucis)*.

A cornerstone of the idealistic view is the conception of man as a being whose growth is determined by the attitude which he assumes toward the reality confronting him. According to the idealistic view, man may be said to lay the foundation of his own existence by the way he orients himself to reality (*operari sequitur esse*, "being follows action"). Against this Luther argues, as we have observed, that what a man does grows out of what he is (*prius est autem esse quam operari*, "being precedes action"). But he also presents the further argument that what a man is results from what he has become, what he has grown to be, what he has suffered and experienced as a recipient of life (*prius autem pati quam esse*, "suffering precedes being").[123]

Suffering Divine Humanness and Impatient Human Godliness

Suffering is one of the fundamental symbols of Luther's thought. Here attention can be focused on it only from a single and quite limited point of view. In opposition to the basic formulation of the traditional view of life, which makes action (*operari*) the basis of being human (*esse*), he presents his view of the rhythm of life in which suffering (*passio, pati*) is the most fundamental experience, that which determines the nature of both being and action. It is in this perspective that he shows man's essential life-orientation to be a listening and obedience to the voice of life. Luther does not deny the importance of living as a disciple of reality, but he claims that man's being is distorted when he considers this attitude to be the essence of humanness and the basic pattern for shaping life. Such an attitude does not prepare man to live or to think in a way that will enable him to confront the deeper aspects of reality toward which one must be more than a mere observer.

The motto of Erasmus, according to Luther,[124] is that man must not think about things that transcend his understanding and that he must learn to revere as divine mystery that which is above him. Erasmus holds that in this area of reality man's reason must submit in obedience to divine revelation.[125] Luther repudiates this attitude, claiming that man confronts divine revelation when he listens to life. Man's conscious attitudes and thoughts are determined by how he "suffers" the speech of life which he does not encounter as an observer. The basic decisions of humanness are made before man responds as a knowing subject to the objective world. They take place on the deeper levels of human existence where man elects with his whole being the affirmation or denial of life. Man's essential choice is whether he consents to unity with the underlying nexus of life or seeks detachment from it, whether he remains in a covenant with life and accepts its bonds of interrelatedness or breaks the covenant and creates his own world.

The subtitle of Luther's reply is "Against the Myth of All the Ages." Luther believes that he is entering into a discussion about an issue in which the whole of human existence is at stake. He is convinced that the view of the essence of being human held both by the traditional humanistic theology (Aristotle) and by the traditional theological humanism (Thomas Aquinas, Erasmus) is contrary to true divine humanness. As Luther conceives it, the nature of this "myth of all the ages" is portrayed in the biblical story of the fall into sin, in which man's denial of life and his estrangement from it are described as a striving for the knowledge of good and evil. According to Luther, a more apt designation for this portrayal would be the "rising" into sin.[126] Man breaks free from obedience to life by his effort to know good and evil, to take hold of life in such a way as to be able to rise above it and to be its observer. The view of life obtained from this position is a "theology of glory," the kind of knowledge of good and evil behind which man barricades himself in order to escape the speech of life.[127]

In taking his stand for confrontation with life upon his own knowledge and choice of position, man shuts himself off from the divine election and the word of life. When Luther speaks about suffering as the precondition of both being and action, he has in mind this situation of being elected and addressed by life. Thus when Erasmus warns Luther against disturbing the peace and insists that the purpose of thinking is to create agreement and harmony among men, Luther replies that thinking which is obedient to the speech of life cannot avoid stirring up conflict and contradiction.[128] In the fortress of his own world man wants to maintain the status quo and to be silent. This man-created world and

its mute gods set themselves against the divine word. Divine
humanness cannot and will not remain silent. To Luther, Erasmus's effort to quiet the storm in which they find themselves is an
attempt to assign to the divine word and revelation its place in
reality and thus control it by means of one's own knowledge.

In his reply to Erasmus, Luther reiterates again and again that
the divine word cannot be bound.[129] Whenever the word of life
confronts man, it acts as a transforming and renewing power.
Man's condition is that of war in which the combatants are divine
humanness and human godliness, living as elect and self-elected
living, spirit and flesh.[130] One of Luther's main arguments against
Erasmus is that his talk about free will leads to a utopian conception of man as a being outside and above the battle going on in
life. He argues that Erasmus's conception of human free will
implies a view of man as a being who is above both life and life's
adversary, a being who is god of gods and lord of lords.

In this context Luther refers to the fact that the Scriptures
speak of God as the God of war and of armies, the Lord Sabaoth,
and that the apostles describe the proclaimers and hearers of the
word as soldiers. The divine is encountered in the kind of humanness in which there is struggle about participation in life, about
acceptance or rejection of being elect. Referring to the words of
Job about human life as warfare, Luther insists that the word of
life itself instigates this warfare.

The Scriptures reveal that the evasion and refusal of life on
the part of man is not an accidental phenomenon. The spirit of
the flesh holds sway not only over some aspect of man but over
man as a whole, not only over some nation but over all mankind.
The air which man breathes comes from the spirit of the flesh.
Men grow into knowledge of good and evil in such a way that
they live and move in it as though it were their own element.
Men become so blinded by their own knowledge of good and
evil, by their own godliness, that they have eyes that do not see
what life is, and ears that do not hear what life says. The light
shines in the darkness. Men consider their sickness to be health.
They do not need a healer and so seek to avoid the touch of the
healing hand. Men regard as authentic life and humanness the

structure of humanity built on their own knowledge of good and evil.

In this knowledge of good and evil men have become interwoven into a web of humanity dominated by supraindividual powers which men have developed and released in the course of their escape from the word of life and their destruction of the unity of life. These powers, described in the Scriptures as the destructive forces of sin, death, law, and wrath, bind men together into an entity bent upon self-destruction. This is the body of humanity controlled by the spirit of the flesh, which the Scriptures describe as having been born of Adam, the man seeking the knowledge of good and evil.

From the midst of this web of mankind spun by human godliness, a new growth springs forth to break and unravel it. It is the living fabric of divine humanness, encompassing all and affecting all just as does the web created by the knowledge of good and evil. The new nexus is described in the Scriptures as the new mankind whose head is the new Adam, Jesus confessed to be the Christ, as the kingdom of heaven, the divine humanity, the chosen people, the church of God.

In depicting man as a battleground on which two kingdoms are engaged in combat, Luther seeks to show that the human predicament is not what Erasmus conceives it to be.[131] Man is wounded in the depth of his being and is in search of healing. Growth into humanness takes place as a transition from sickness to health,[132] as a deliverance of conscience shackled by the powers of condemnation into freedom to hear the speech of life, as a transformation of the web of guilt into the fabric of grace.

Luther describes man's basic condition as crucifixion.[133] With its knowledge of good and evil, mankind has crucified itself. The cruciform shape of human existence is revealed in all its depth in the crucified Jesus. Crossing each other in him are the web of the knowledge of good and evil, which suppresses life, and the network of grace which brings forth life from beneath death, sin, law, and wrath. Every man experiences this cross in his own being, and by the way he relates himself to his cross he makes the supreme decision of his life.

Luther notes that when Erasmus speaks of the ability of free will to attach itself to what is good, he presupposes that man knows what is best for him. But in the light of the gospel it is clear that death and all manner of evil in the world may serve man best in leading him from the power of death into life. Thus if man had the kind of free will that Erasmus speaks about, it is death that he should will. Erasmus speaks about the divine as a reality operating only within what man himself with his knowledge of good and evil regards as good. To Luther the divine word is contained within everything that happens (*tota creatura verbum dei*, "everything created is the word of God").

Man's knowledge of good and evil must not be allowed to determine what divine humanness is. Luther stresses that the divine is encountered as the cross which breaks the hold of the powers that suppress the growth of life. Divine humanness breaks forth to expose the pretensions of human godliness, which aspires to be the judge and determiner of life. As love goes into action it stirs up the forces of hate, doing mercy unveils the violence rooted in man's being, faith calls forth the resistance of unfaith. The divine is thus concealed beneath its opposites (*sub contraria specie*, "under the aspect of the contrary").[134]

The realization of humanness thus takes place in a situation of distress which calls a man to become a man of conscience responding to the speech of life. Humanness is realized as a continuous dividing of spirits, the separation of the spirit of life from the spirit of the flesh. From this standpoint Luther emphasizes the importance of the continuous use of the word and the sacraments. Conscience can grow only through constant attention to the living word which divides the spirits. If Erasmus were right, Luther exclaims, then the condition of the world could be changed by a single act of preaching the divine word. But the basic situation of human life is such that men must put on the whole armor and make use of the whole arsenal of weapons afforded by the experiences of men obedient to the word of life. Man must learn to live in a state of openness, listening to the speech of life, not drawing from his own knowledge of good and evil the standards for judging between right and wrong prophecy.

With his dialectic of law and gospel, as indicated above, Luther seeks to lead man to become a listener to the word of life. The fundamental tension of human experience is the distress which man experiences in his conscience when he is aware on the one hand of the promise inherent in his life and on the other hand of the judgment and threat also present. Within man's being, a mortal combat goes on between the man of good conscience and the man of evil conscience, between the man living by promise and the man terrified by judgment and seeking refuge in law. From this tension in his being man cannot set himself free. He has no escape from the distress occasioned by the clash between experienced promise and the attendant threat of judgment. A man must grow to be a man of conscience and learn to distinguish in himself between what is sustained by promise and what is threatened by judgment. No man is permitted to transfer to another this task of dividing the gospel and the law, the promise and the judgment.

As man seeks to escape this distressing freedom, this suffering which is education for divine humanness, he evades sharing in divine creativity. Man has been created to live in creative change, in metamorphosis. In evading this he becomes a being who only conforms to the various situations of life and who is determined by the various external conditions of reality. He becomes a man "under the law," one who fulfills not the promise inherent in his being but laws outside himself. Under the law man is estranged from his own being and uses some law or other to suppress his own inner sensibilities. Man thus loses his conscience and allows something else to become his conscience.

Luther speaks of the theology of the cross as training for participation in the creativity of divine patience and suffering. In linking together thinking and suffering, he does not idealize submissive and passive suffering as is the case with the traditional "imitation of Christ." Suffering-thinking is creative and stretches toward the future. It is not afraid to face violence and destruction, that which in the form of death ultimately confronts everything human. The crucifixion and resurrection of Jesus show that death does not have the last word, that the word of life breaks through and tears apart the web made out of the knowledge of good and evil, that life springs forth and shatters the artificial worlds built on the knowledge of good and evil. The theology of the cross is exercise in thinking according to the rhythm of crucifixion and resurrection, the death of the old and the springing forth of the new.[135]

One of the most important differences between Luther and Erasmus is that Erasmus clings to the past while Luther stretches forward to grasp the future. Erasmus sees danger threatening not only the church but all of Western culture as the earthquake of violent upheaval breaks down the prevailing forms of social life and the accustomed ways of thought. Erasmus does his utmost to stay clear of this tragic course of events. Luther, on the contrary, is convinced that the earthquake serves the purpose of destroying suppressive petrified forms of life and thought and preparing the way for what is to come, the life of a new humanity.

Erasmus views Christianity in the perspective of the past as a tradition spreading through mankind, a legacy to be preserved for posterity. Luther, on the contrary, views it as the new humanity that is to come, the promised land toward which mankind, liberated from bondage, is traveling. Erasmus conceives of Christianity primarily as the church, the society born out of the influence of Christ and his apostles and gradually extending over the whole earth. Luther, on the other hand, prefers to use such expressions as *Christian folk* or *Christendom (heilige Christenheit)*. He speaks of it as a net enclosing all generations and all mankind from one end of the earth to the other, an interlacing of human life which heralds the appearance of true humanity.

When Luther speaks of the theology of the cross as a way of thinking which teaches one to regard punishment, cross, and death as precious treasures,[136] he is not merely using poetic expressions or engaging in spiritual meditation. He speaks about hard tangible facts and calls for exercise in the kind of thinking which is open to things that are contrary to a man's own attitudes. When a man barricades himself behind positions furnished by his own knowledge of good and evil, he selects as the content of his thought only those elements of reality which fit into the world created by his knowledge. Yet it is precisely in what shatters rudely his own attitudes and thoughts that the word of life is concealed. Divine humanness breaks forth as a power that crushes inhumanness, divine love is experienced as an anger that overcomes lovelessness. Only thinking which faces up to the cruciform nature of reality remains open to reality. Only a man nailed on the cross contained in the basic condition of being human can become detached from the old and share in the creation of the new, in the resurrection of life from death. Just as the Scriptures conclude with the prayer "Come, Lord Jesus,"[137] a prayer reaching for divine humanness, so the experience of man and of mankind leads to a quest for the humanity that is to come.

Chapter Three

Openness to What Is to Come

Humanness becomes a basic language symbol especially in revolutionary times when the established social forms crumble.[1] Revolution generally contains deep humanistic pathos. Prevailing forms of life and thought are battered down in the name of humanity. Critical periods in social life also give rise to anthropological research which seeks to explain the essential human predicament. When the institutional structures of society lose the authority which the members of society have held to be self-evident, and when man thus becomes a problem and a riddle to himself, investigation on what it means to be a man is engendered.

Our time has often been described as the century of anthropology. It is indeed obvious that Western culture is marked by numerous indications that man has become a riddle to himself and is also reexamining his social institutions. In a variety of forms the idea is being expressed that "the human" has been "excommunicated," pushed outside the established forms of life and thought. This argument comes most sharply to the fore in communistic thinking and action.[2] Western industrialization is said to have dehumanized man's behavior and thought to such a degree that humanness cannot develop unless the established institutions are destroyed. Allegedly those who in the course of industrial development have acquired positions of ownership are determined in their thinking on man by the effort to defend their positions. Only the proletariat, which has experienced the inhumanity of the structures of life built upon the acquisitive motive in the industrial process, is capable of free and creative thought and action in the name of authentic humanity. All other thinking is rationalization of positions of ownership. Only he who has suffered in his own being the exploitation of humanness by the prevailing orders is enabled to think clearly and to have insight into the true causes of the dehumanization. Estrangement from humanness takes place collectively rather than individually. It is brought about by the shaping of the institutional structures of life together. It is there that man's inhumanity to man becomes manifest, and only those who have experienced this inhumanity most deeply can be the heralds of true humanity. They have the power of thought and action to overthrow the established institutional structures. The humanizing of society cannot be achieved merely by educating individuals. Inhumanity has become ingrained in the institutions which men have created, and only by the creation of truly human social structures is the possibility afforded for the growth of humanness in individuals. Conscious thinking on the part of individuals does not determine the nature of their existence. It is their membership or lack of membership in the community that determines their consciousness. In summoning men to overthrow the economic structures which dominate the productive life of the group, the communist manifesto champions humanity and calls for a radical reexamination of the basic situation of being human.

The Marxist anthropology is an example of the kind of approach which holds that in principle the problem of humanness has been solved. Marxism has selected as its starting point a specific interpretation of the fundamental human predicament. On the other hand, that part of the Western world which strives to construct the forms of social life in vital interaction of its total heritage has made freedom its watchword. While freedom is here defined in countless different ways, on one principle there is general agreement. It is this: human life must not be molded to conform to one single ideal.[3] As the starting point of thought and action one must not select an isolated conception of what it means to be human. Only an existence realized in the spirit of exploration is worthy of a human being.

In the first section of this study the nature of the spirit of exploration was briefly sketched. It was also noted that this spirit is threatened on two sides. On the one hand is a type of religion and theology of revelation which sets up a concept of the nature of divine reality as the criterion of everything human (positivism of revelation). On the other hand is the attempt to control life in the name of science, in which a concept of the nature of human experience is made the standard of reality. The explorer must sail through the narrows of such a Scylla and Charybdis if he is to continue his quest. The second main section was an analysis of a phase of this quest in an age which in its violence and revolution bears much resemblance to our own time. The analysis indicated the dangers that must be faced. The straits which the explorer has to navigate contain such perilous eddies that he is tempted either to retreat or to stop and do battle with the opposing forces. The former alternative may be designated as the temptation to skeptical relativism in which the peril is evaded and the voyage continues on less troubled waters. The latter may be described as the temptation to an absolutism which resorts to the enemy's own weapons as it seeks to overcome the monstrous forces that terrorize life.

The third main section will attempt to focus attention on matters which are essential to the effort to escape the alternatives of absolutism and relativism. Thus this section is in fact a continuation of the study of man as explorer. The method is still an analysis of concepts.

The kind of philosophy which concentrates on the basic meaning of humanness, the thinking that seeks wisdom for living, has since the days of Socrates been compared to the work of a physician. Wittgenstein[4] says, "The philosopher's treatment of a question is like the treatment of an illness." Illness has to be approached with a variety of methods; there is no single method for curing it. This applies also to the study of man. No single approach may be regarded as the only method for research on man. In analyzing the fundamental condition of being human one cannot proceed therefore from only one concept of man. In speaking of his work as a philosopher Wittgenstein affirms that he has no philosophical opinions. The task of the philosopher is to free the human mind from the grip of confusion. A thinker who allows some problem to captivate his mind is in a dreamlike condition. The purpose of philosophy is to provide an awakening from this dream, to free the mind from the problem which holds it captive. "What is your aim in philosophy? To show the fly the way out of the fly-bottle" (Wittgenstein). The purpose of conceptual analysis is to give the human mind freedom to think. Specific alternatives selected by the thinking process—images and ideas— imprison the mind. The language that a man uses may obstruct the exploration of creative thinking. Language may become petri- fied into fixed concepts and alternatives which repeatedly drive the mind into a labyrinth from which there is no escape. A therapeutic method of thinking is afforded by an analytical study of language which seeks through concepts contact with the vari- eties of the world of experience and which through its configura- tions attempts to direct action within it.

Disturbances in Speaking about the Divine and the Human

An object lesson of the crisis of our culture, manifest in current thought and speech concerning the divine and the human, is fur- nished by the Montreal world exposition, Expo 67.[5] It expresses powerfully the understanding of life and reality characteristic of our generation. The theme of the exposition, "Man and His World," was selected at the beginning of the past decade by a group of Canadian scholars. The theme was inspired by the book *The World of Man (Terre des Hommes)* by Antoine de Saint- Exupéry. The group of men which made the preparations for the exposition sought to bring together representatives of the various areas of life from all parts of the world to deal with the question: What is man?

The scholars who worked on the theme of Expo 67 held that the philosophy of the exposition might be summed up in the words of the man from whom they drew their inspiration: "To be a man means to feel that one is making a contribution toward helping to build a world." The aim of Expo, according to those who set it up, was to furnish the opportunity to examine man in the total field of his behavior. To achieve this goal man was viewed in three perspectives in accordance with the three sub- divisions of the main theme. The primary purpose was to call the viewers to look upon man as a creative being ("Man the Creator," *le génie createur de l'homme*). To the men who formulated the Expo theme it was especially important to display the capabilities inherent in human nature for creative art as well as for originality in planning the industrial world. The second subtheme was "Man in the Community" *(l'homme dans la cité)*. The purpose of the pavilions exhibiting it was to set forth human interdependence in various groups and in the whole fabric of mankind. The third perspective for examining man was the point of view of exploration, man as investigator and inventor ("Man the Explorer," *l'homme interroge l'universe*). Beside the pavilions representing these central motifs were two other thematic displays closely related to "Man the Explorer": man as producer and man as cultivator of the earth.

Vitally related to these thematic pavilions and expressing the slogan of the exposition in a most important way was a windowless five-story building called the labyrinth. Its theme was the Theseus legend of Greek mythology. The labyrinth conducted the viewer through the various phases of human life: birth, childhood, confident youth, doubt, confusion, and finally regeneration. In the last chamber man the hero confronted a beast that was trying to destroy humanity. The labyrinth sought to lead the traveler in the maze to find the sources of true humanness in his own being and to draw from them courage to confront the beast lurking within himself.

The Christian churches of Canada accepted together the invitation to participate in the presentation of the theme of the exposition. The Protestant, Roman Catholic, and Orthodox churches decided to join in constructing a pavilion having no traditional Christian symbols. It had no pictures of churches, no religious slogans or works of art, no sermons, hymns, or prayers. It did not try to explain anything. The visitor was led along without a chance to stop, just as a man walks in daily life. The theme of the pavilion, "The Eighth Day," expressed the day of man on earth. The viewer was conducted through three sections. The first one expressed the "heartbeats" of human life through photographs taken in various situations in which people were unaware that their actions were being observed. The second section with its low ceiling brought the visitor face to face with man's inhumanity to man. In its darkness was shown a film of the violence which man has done during the past half-century to himself, to his fellowmen, and to his environment. The last section portrayed the reality of the resurrection in the midst of human life: children at play, youth in love, adults rejoicing in one another, old people with a gleam of humor and hope in their eyes. The pavilion opened toward the whole area of the exposition, summoning the viewer to see the presence of the divine in the midst of daily human existence.

Expo's Christian pavilion was an attempt to transmit without traditional symbols the traditional Christian message of the manifestation of divine humanness in Jesus, whom Christians confess to be the Christ. The traditional Christian churches here spoke the same language and used the same symbols as the other pavilions dealing with the exposition theme, the nature of man. For example, the labyrinth and the Christian pavilion sounded the same note in many respects.

The Christian pavilion in a world impelled by the exploring spirit of Expo 67 is a telling example of the condition described in the first section of our study. It shows the situation of theology in the research and discussion dealing with the man of today and his world. This is especially evident in the reactions which the joint pavilion of the Christian churches aroused in various parts of the theological world.[6] On the one hand, the pavilion and the theology underlying it were accused of being unfaithful to divine revelation and the Christian tradition. Critics who held this view charged that the pavilion, like the rest of Expo, spoke only of man and his world, leaving out God and his world. Some Christian groups erected their own pavilion which proclaimed the allegedly excluded divine message. Their purpose was to bring the divine revelation into a world that was indifferent to it. On the other hand, the Christian pavilion was acclaimed as an expression of the heart of the Christian faith as it seeks to communicate the incarnation of the divine in the human. From this point of view the Christian pavilion, together with other pavilions faith-

ful to the theme of the exposition, has been regarded as a pro-
claimer of the creative and redemptive presence of the divine in
all of human life.

The discussion concerning Expo's Christian pavilion is a concrete example of the crisis in which Western Christian groups
find themselves as they deal with the subject of God and man.
The pavilion brought to light the fact that men have come to
speak two different languages, one in the church and the other
in the everyday world. The men who set up the pavilion realized
that in the explorerlike context of Expo the only way in which
they could speak about the presence of the divine in human life
was to use language entirely different from that of the church.

The discussion aroused by the Christian pavilion affords a new
point of view for understanding this fragmentation of language.
The conflicting reactions to the attempt of Christian churches at
a united ecumenical communication of the message of the gospel
by means of universal human symbols do not follow denominational lines. From within the same denomination have risen theological judgments both of sharp condemnation and of approval.
This indicates that the present crisis does not involve language difficulties between different Christian language groups; the language common to the same group is being fragmented.[7] It is
evident that the contradictions and disagreements between
denominations are not so disruptive as the differences between
those who speak the same religious language and yet accuse one
another of heresy and apostasy. Groups which label one another
as fundamentalists or liberals are drifting into a situation in which
there are not only differing views on the nature of the encounter
between the divine and the human but various groups thoroughly
and radically questioning and rejecting each other's views.
Obviously the Scylla and Charybdis of the present moment represent the temptation described above to become entrenched in the
contradiction between absolutism and relativism. This division
constitutes a greater threat to Christianity than the division of
Christendom into various denominations.

We have examined a controversy during the days of the Reformation, which concerned a similar crisis of Christian language
and which severely tested the unity of western Christendom. It

became evident that the crisis in religious language reflected a general crisis taking place in the society of that day. Many signs are pointing to the fact that the fragmentation of religious language experienced by our generation reflects an extensive change in communal life, which is causing in various areas the same kind of fragmentation of language and search for a new language as we see in the churches. In the research on man this division into separate networks of language is manifest, for example, in the studies which create theories for the education or the healing of man. Studies of man from a biological, psychological, sociological, historical, or philosophical point of view take place for the most part in their own spheres of language without intercommunication. In these separate worlds is manifest, as we shall seek to show, the same congealment into positions of absolutism and relativism as in the sphere of theological discussion.

Our analysis of the controversy between Luther and Erasmus indicates that these fragmentations of language, these disruptions in communication, do not have merely a negative character. The breakdown of language may contain new possibilities of growth. In his medical study of the anthropology of speech and speech disturbances, Martti Siirala demonstrates that in the treatment of children's speech disturbances amazing sources of healing may be discovered by listening to the search for wholeness, contained in the disturbance. The more advanced the speech difficulty, he affirms, the clearer it becomes that the center of the therapeutic problem is somewhere other than in the speech itself. "A disease process is constantly eloquent in some way: it is sounding an alarm, or at least giving a reminder, concerning an aspect of life that is threatened by distortion or suffocation. . . . Clearly, the symptom becomes increasingly remote as an appeal, the more its message is ignored; at the same time it becomes more massive from the point of view of the individual. Its quality as an address is progressively lost as hope diminishes. (The connotations of 'hope', here, are complex: they include hope that a sense of common responsibility for the dilemma will be awakened; hope that personal responsibility will be restored; hope of relieving the diseased organ of a burden that does not belong to it; hope of growth.) . . . Thus the causes of human diseases and defects cannot ever be entirely beyond human responsibility and guilt. They are inseparable from man's obligation to his life for his specific being, his indebtedness. The spatially and temporally specified causal events that we have verified are always *selections*. They have been isolated from the wider historical configurations of certain dimensions of human existence. These wider configurations must, however, be brought into view if we wish to set a healing process in motion— a new integration, and not the mere elimination of a narrowly defined defect, curtailed in both space and time. Traditionally, medicine has tended to favour two stands concerning cause: either the cause is an unchanged and unchangeable irreversibility; or it is an eradicable defect, an evil that has been unearthed from concealment and must be removed from the scene. The causes whereby diseases and defects originate and are maintained are not readily seen as containing any hidden productive possibilities. And yet the experience in extended, long-term treatment makes it increasingly clear that a substantial improvement always means more than the mere disappearance of some defect or detriment: it means the discovery of sources and potentialities that were previously concealed."[8]

The following is an attempt to sketch a procedure for finding the way out of the impasse of a discussion which leads to the alternatives of absolutism and relativism.

Cruciform Reality

We are truly a remarkable generation in that we live violently and arouse hatred, and yet consider peace and the construction of sound human relations as the central aim of our endeavors. In our reports about life we use most frequently the words *violence* and *revolution*. Within the sphere of western Christendom we have destroyed in recent decades tens of millions of our fellow-men and immeasurable areas of the works of human hands as well as of nature. We have seen the spirit of violence and revolution gain a foothold in large areas of the most sensitive human associations. In the relations between children and parents, young people and adults, students and teachers, women and men, we observe violent mutual opposition and impatient rebellion.[9] Even cancer, the specific disease of our era,[10] manifests a violation of the fabric of life. At the same time we experience in our generation in countless concrete ways our belongingness to a many-fibered and rich fabric of humanity. We are in increasingly rewarding interaction with both past generations and various human communities of our own time. We feel in our own being the life of humanity. We have the experience of being bound together in many ways with men endeavoring to bring about peace and mutual understanding. Just as hardly any generation can compete with ours in violence, so likewise it is hard to find another generation in which so much dedicated work has been done for the cause of peace.

The most tragic aspect of the situation is that the more we make progress in building bridges, the wider are the chasms between human groups. The hungry become hungrier and the well-fed better fed, the poor become poorer and the rich richer, the rebellious become more rebellious and the ones in power more violent toward the rebels. In this situation it becomes more and more difficult to isolate the reality of violence and wars as something fortuitous, as blind fate that draws into its vortex men who are striving for peace and progress. It is also difficult to attribute the cause of violence and wars any longer to barbarians who hardly deserve to be called men. This holds true particularly of us who have grown into manhood in the midst of western Christendom. Our past history and our present day are especially violent and warlike. We cannot evade the question of the relation between our Christian-humanistic tradition and the outgrowth of violence within it. We are compelled to acknowledge in increasing measure that violence and hate belong to our own being and that the wars going on in our midst are our wars. It becomes ever more apparent that we share in many ways in the violence and the fighting. Our experience shows that we are engaged in creating the kind of peace and humanness which at the same time generates wars and inhumanness.

In this distressing situation, in which we experience the inseparable interlocking of good and evil, life and death, health and sickness, love and hate, peace and war, and humanness and inhumanness, it becomes more and more difficult for us to take refuge in the fortresses of the knowledge of good and evil afforded by our tradition. We see not only the inadequacy of all available concepts of man as directives in the present situation but also the untenability of the whole approach that seeks to shape life in accordance with fixed concepts of man. In such a situation it is easy to resort to an absolutizing of some ideological, religious, or scientific view of life which enables us to escape the contradiction of existence. Another alternative is a neurotic existentialism in which the starting point and the total perspective is an analysis of the distress we experience. The result is the impasse described above in which a battle line is drawn between an idealistic objectivism and collectivism on the one side and an antiidealistic individualism and subjectivism on the other.

In the beginning of this study the hypothesis was presented that the experience of reality in terms of an encounter between the divine and the human, expressed in speech about God and things divine, makes a significant contribution to the study of man conducted in the spirit of exploration. In the light of the analysis made in the second main section it became clear that this contribution consists in pointing out that life's basic associations are of central importance in defining humanness. How life is realized in the unifying connections in which man is dependent on the soil of his growth and on his fellowmen is decisive in the process of becoming human.[11]

The importance of these unifying factors may be clarified by following the procedure suggested by the German-American sociologist and philosopher Eugen Rosenstock-Huessy[12] as he describes the basic structure of humanness. Rosenstock-Huessy is one of the few thinkers of our time who have focused their thought and research upon listening to what wars, revolutions, and manifestations of violence have to say on the meaning of humanness. In presenting his description of the fundamental human predicament he refers to the words of Winston Churchill, a man of our generation who experienced deeply the meaning of violence: "A man's life must be nailed to a cross either of thought or of action."[13] The reality of human life, according to Rosenstock-Huessy, is cruciform. Our life is realized in a continuing experience of conflict, in a combat between opposing forces, in endurance and suffering in the midst of tendencies pulling us in opposite directions. As temporal beings we must face at the same time both the past and the future. No one lives only in one time. At every moment we shape again our past and our future. In the same way, we live as spatial beings simultaneously in an inner and in an outer world. In our individual and collective life our own inner world and community takes shape together with its external reality. Our individual and social life is realized on four fronts extending in as many directions: backward toward the past, forward toward the future, inward toward living in our own being and community, and outward toward what we must learn to control or to what we must submit, what we must struggle against or what we must use to our advantage.

As the intersection of these four basic dimensions, human life is realized in constant examination of what is to be allowed to continue and what is to be overcome or changed, in constant search for the boundary between the inner reality in which we live in continuous dialogue with ourselves and with our fellow-men and the external world which is the object of our speech, thought, and action. No one's individual experience or thought is adequate for this analysis. It requires interaction and division of labor. Some of us, as teachers, clergymen, or lawyers, concentrate on clarifying or constructing our relation to the past and on searching for ways of maintaining a right continuity of life. Others, as poets, artists, and musicians, help us to cultivate the interconnections of the inner life in all its diversified nuances. Still others, as scientists, do battle for us on the external front where the effort is made to protect life by learning to control the forces of nature and to use them to serve the common good. There are also prophets and statesmen among us who summon us to change our habits of thought and patterns of life and to be open to the future.

Within the framework of these dimensions we shall examine contemporary research on man with a view to pointing out some aspects which tend to be overlooked when man is regarded primarily as a disciple of reality. Attention must be concentrated on the point of intersection where growth into humanness takes place in a tension between tendencies directed inward and those directed outward. Only incidental reference can be made to humanness as a tension between the past and the future, for the material presented in the main section of our study sheds little light on this aspect.

Contemporary study of man views him chiefly as a disciple of reality and tends to disregard the fundamental interrelatedness of life. This is evident in the separateness of the various fields of anthropological study, to which reference has already been made. There is a strong tendency to carry on research in various areas and on various levels without mutual confrontation. Paul Tillich[14] points out that this stratification in the study of man is based on the view of nature as a hierarchical organization. Reality is regarded as a pyramid with inorganic, organic, psychological, and other strata, each representing a different grade of the power and worth of existence. Originally the hierarchy stood for an order of sacred rulers, in which each had his place in accordance with the kind of sacramental power which he represented. This picture of the hierarchy of rulers *(arkhoi)* signifies that the higher levels are considered to be qualitatively nobler as well as quantitatively fewer. At the apex is a single monarch, a supreme being, the god of a world view or of a monotheistic religion.

This hierarchical view of nature and of human reality contains the idea that between the different strata there is no organic interaction. There is interaction only through control and the reaction to control. Particularly fateful, according to Tillich, is the result of the use of the concept of levels in explaining the relation between the psychic and the spiritual. If the body and the soul are regarded as levels, the study of this relation leads to fruitless alternatives. Either the spiritual is reduced to a manifestation of life on the organic level (biologism, psychologism) or else it is considered to be a separate factor having its own influence upon life on the biological and psychological level.

Tillich claims that this thinking in terms of levels is also evident in the way in which the relation between culture and religion is understood in our Western communities. Culture is conceived to be a level on which man exercises his own creativity. Religion, on the other hand, is a level on which man receives divine revelation about himself and about reality. Religion is thus seen as exercising control over culture, and creative culture is rebellion against this control. The divine and the human are thus realities which are situated on different levels. The divine and the religious represent supernatural reality, while the cultural and the human pertain to human reason and experience.

In analyzing the differences between the concepts *level* and *dimension* Tillich says that every metaphorical assertion has a twofold connotation, drawing its content both from the sector of reality from which it is taken and from the reality which it is used to describe. Both *level* and *dimension* are derived from the world of space, and they are used to express the total structure of reality. When the hypothetical starting points in the interpretation of reality are the encountered contradictions and tensions, it is natural to select *level* as the basic expression. The nature of reality is so described that what occurs in it is explicable in terms of the tensions prevailing between its levels. But if the interpretation of reality proceeds from the hypothesis that life forms a unity, then *dimension* is a more suitable expression than *level*, for various dimensions may meet and intersect one another without involving contradiction.

In describing life as a multidimensional unity, Tillich seeks to show that the ambiguities of life do not result from various levels of content and that the ambiguity of reality is not overcome by any specific hierarchy of levels. These ambiguities are contained in life itself in all its dimensions. They are not attributable to tensions between various strata. Life itself is ambiguous.

Man as Child of Life and Molder of Life

Descartes,[15] whose influence in laying the foundation for contemporary thinking on the nature of man excels that of any other architect of modern thought, complains that man has a long period of childhood during which the human mind receives impressions without being able to exercise rational control over them. It is unfortunate, he says, that the first two decades of human life are spent in a situation in which man does not understand what is happening to him. Instead of being equipped on the threshold of adulthood with a clear brain, he has to use up much of his energy at this stage to root out erroneous images and ideas. It is deplorable that man cannot think clearly from the time of his birth and that man's consciousness contains memories from a period when in fact he was not yet a man. According to Descartes, authentic human existence may be traced to the moment when man's thinking obtains a hold on rationally controlled reality: *cogito, ergo sum* ("I think, therefore I am"). The ideal man is an empty subject which is gradually filled with objectivity. Man must therefore learn to sever his relation to his childhood and to forget it. One must assume an attitude of doubt toward everything that binds him to the original situation of life. Doubt is the fundamental prerequisite of true humanness, rationality. All personal and social connections must be eliminated from thinking.

There are some noteworthy resemblances between Erasmus and Descartes in life and in personality. Their attitudes toward the child and childhood and their attempts to set up the doubting observer as the ideal for orientation to reality have biographical backgrounds. Erasmus[16] was born outside of wedlock, the son of a man who was later pressured by his parents into becoming a priest, and his mother died when he was still very young. His relatives hustled him off into a monastery, and when he reached adulthood he found himself in the garb of an Augustinian monk. His feelings about life are clearly set forth in his tract on the foolishness of men, *Encomium moriae*. He describes men as greedy, vain, and ignorant, and he asks why time should be wasted in the name of rational deity to change the human race into something that it does not want to be. Descartes, for his part, sought deliberately to live in isolation from other men. He had no family, and he fled from all social relations. When, for example, he lived for two decades in a society in which his mother tongue was not spoken, he refrained from learning the language of the land in order to remain as isolated as possible. In an age of religious wars Descartes belonged to an aristocracy which lived its own life above other people and the circumstances in which they were involved. This isolation was broken only by a fortuitous episode which led him to bear responsibility for a child who lived a few years.

Descartes, like Erasmus, was a divided personality in the sense that he considered doubt to be the mother of clear thinking and yet was obedient to the patriarchal authority of the church. This man who sought passionately to obtain a clear and distinct understanding of reality *(clara et distincta perceptio rerum)* made a pilgrimage to the home of the Virgin Mary, which was said to have been carried by angels from Palestine to Italy, and wrote in defense of the church's doctrine of the transubstantiation of the elements of the Eucharist. He resembles Erasmus also in that he made a deliberate effort to concentrate on his own scholarly work and to avoid public controversy. When Galileo was before the Inquisition, only a few of his scientific colleagues came to his defense. Descartes too refused to become involved, although he could have done it without much danger, for he was financially independent and lived in a land that was out of the reach of the Inquisition. When he was asked to express his attitude toward Galileo, who was then already under arrest, his reply was exceedingly cautious. He expressed himself in such a way that no one could accuse him of contradicting the creation story of the Bible.

We have referred to the status of the child and of childhood in the thought and life of these two men because here we face concretely a fundamental issue in the educational and industrial world of our society. While Erasmus and Descartes follow lines of thought which are quite divergent in many respects, their common trait is a strong conviction of the rational nature of reality and a view of man as disciple of this reality. They represent a way of thinking which has given rise to unique technological development.

The progress of technology has provided empirical verification of the power of the kind of theoretical and abstract thinking which strives for impersonal objective knowledge. Science based on such thinking has gradually risen in our society into the same position of authority as the church had in the medieval community. When universally valid ideas and knowledge that is free from subjectivity are regarded as the most reliable contact with reality, authority belongs to the men who know the reality of ideas and are masters of objective knowledge. Knowledge is simultaneously the basic virtue and the highest authority. The hierarchy of values and of men in the community takes shape in accordance with how deeply and how extensively a value or a man shares in the universally valid content of reality. These universally valid elements themselves are the actual authority. They operate with the power of their own gravity.

To regard such knowledge as the most reliable and to strive to achieve it by the strictest possible exclusion of man's subjective experience leads to a social structuring in which the community represents objectivity and plays the role of absolute authority among its members. The nature of the welfare of the members of the community is defined in terms of the knowledge which is dominant at the moment.

When man's growth and self-knowledge are considered to be determined by how he relates himself to the laws of reality, the central task of education for humanness becomes socialization, the unification of man with the community which represents the rationality of reality and its implicit divine or natural order. The classical expression of this view is Plato's ideal state. In describing *paideia*, Plato's ideal of education, Jaeger[17] shows that it is based on his rational theology. The foundation for this theology was laid by the philosophers of nature who undertook the analysis of the laws of nature and the basic principles of existence. They did away with the mythical anthropomorphic deities of the Greek tradition. This bold speculative philosophizing which sought to obtain a rational hold on the highest and most difficult issues of life lost its strength, however, as the Sophists turned away from all speculation to concentrate in a spirit of skepticism upon the practical questions of human education. The Sophists rejected the study of the divine principles of reality and without any metaphysical system confined themselves to an empirical study of man's individual and social life. Socrates with his famous questions closed this road. He showed, Jaeger continues, that true education is not concerned merely with training in methods of thinking and learning. Education presupposes a quest for awareness of the ends to which man is to be led. It also presupposes certainty of the good which it seeks to attain. From this point of view the assertion of the Sophists that man is the measure of all things meant a declaration of bankruptcy of human culture. Plato uses the ideas of Socrates to express his own pedagogical effort, the attempt to show that the line of development which begins with the practical questions of education and virtue leads eventually to a confrontation with the divine principle of reality. Plato calls this principle absolute. In his book on laws Plato declares that God is the measure of all things. True *paideia*, whether it concerns education or legislation, is based on God as the highest norm. Its purpose is to convert man from the delusions of the world of sense into participation in the divine world which contains the absolute good and the highest goal of all human striving. Thus in Plato's ideal state capital punishment is decreed for atheists.

According to Aristotle,[18] likewise, growth into humanness takes place as incorporation into a community in which the ideals implicit in reality are realized. He sees the Greek city-state *(polis)* as such a community. It brings order into the chaos of human instincts.

A large part of the structuring of Western society has taken place as a result of this basic idealistic view. When the core of reality is thought to consist of the ideals and laws which it contains, the effort is made to order society by means of institutional structures which protect and educate human life through laws, conceived as either natural or supernatural. In this way the institutions of a society stand for reason as against arbitrariness, health as against sickness, the divine or natural order as against the chaos of the senses and the instincts. The community with its institutional forms is healthier than its individual members.

Built upon this idealistic foundation are countless varying forms of communal life which seek in different ways to determine the relation between society and the individual. In analyzing the structure of the idealistic formation of society, the American sociologist Philip Rieff[19] points out that its varieties manifest a common basic feature. To the idealistic view it is impossible to conceive of such a distortion of the collective forms of life that society would cease to represent objectivity and rationality for the individual.

As we have observed in the preceding section of our study, Luther endeavored in his thought and action to free himself from the questions of the idealistic tradition. He sought in a radical way to show that the institutions of society can become pathological and destructive in such measure as to require their overthrow by the fundamental vitalities and the word of life. Luther's insights into the pathology of society and its institutions have been largely disregarded. For the most part the revolution against the idealistic structuring of society has occurred under the banner of antiidealistic individualism.

In portraying the individualistic movement which looks upon society as an obstacle to the growth of the individual and seeks to clear the way for humanness through radical isolation from society, Rieff refers to de Tocqueville's description of a truly free democratic man. True democracy summons its adherent to detach himself from the mass of his fellowmen, from family and friends, and to engage in the formation of groups of creative individuals, which are to provide training for liberation from collective ways of feeling and thinking. True democracy not only leads a man to forget his ancestors but also hides his progeny from him and separates him from his contemporaries. It casts a man into utter self-dependence and threatens to incarcerate him finally in the solitary confinement of his own heart. A democratic man owes no one anything and expects nothing from anyone. He forges his own fortune.

In his study of the sources of radically individualistic democratic thought, F. S. C. Northrop calls John Locke the architect of this ideology.[20] Locke applied to man the new theory of nature set forth by Newton and Galileo. Unlike Descartes, he did not proceed from doubting everything but constructed his view

on verified scientific theory, which gave him the key for understanding man and his conscious life. Just as nature is assembled
from atomlike material substances, so men are separate mental
substances reacting to nature. This reaction engenders various
moral, religious, and political attitudes. Man as a physical being
belongs to nature composed of material atoms. As a mental being,
however, he is completely free from material substance. As he is
a mental entity, his conscious existence is shaped in complete
independence also from fellowmen. Human individuals have no
organic connection with one another. The growth of a human
individual does not depend on the existence of other men. Man is
thus a completely autonomous and self-dependent being. Nature
contains no laws to govern relations between men. The laws of
all communities have the character of agreements between men.
Their authority and content are determined entirely by what
autonomous individuals make of them. The church, like society
itself, is a community voluntarily formed by men. No one is
born to be its member. Religion is altogether a man's private
affair. The soul care of each man belongs to himself alone. The
prerequisite of growth into humanness is an atmosphere in which
men have a spirit of tolerance and acknowledge one another as
free and independent, as separate students of reality.

Individualism of this type, constructing its view of the human
and the divine upon a view of nature which supplanted the
Aristotelian philosophy of nature, led to a denial of the social
substance of life which had been strongly emphasized both in
ancient idealistic philosophy and in scholastic theology. In this
respect Luther's thought with its effort to explicate life's basic
associations follows an entirely different line from that of individualism. On the other hand, the protest against the idealistic
structuring of society, raised by the therapeutic movement
pioneered by Sigmund Freud, contains features quite similar to
Luther's attack on the idealistic tradition.[21]

In the social structuring which is built on the ideal of objectivity and in which the knowledge that man gathers from reality
is the measure of man's worth, the ignorant are neglected or
actually excommunicated. It is no accident that in the first

stage of industrialization it was the children above all who suffered, or that the least knowledgeable became the proletariat, or that those who were mentally disturbed and thus unwilling to adjust to the dominant process of knowing were isolated and persecuted.

When Freud set himself to listen to the mentally ill, whom society had largely left without attention or care, he soon incurred scorn from his colleagues and others close to him. But his therapeutic efforts were opposed also from another direction. He encountered in the sick persons who sought care a conscious or unconscious resistance to getting well. In analyzing this phenomenon, Gustaf Bally, Swiss philosopher and psychoanalyst, affirms that these patients fled from healing because they did not want to get well in the way prescribed by the community. They sought another kind of health and another way to health than the one offered by the community. Freud listened to their search and discovered in the illness of his patients deep suspicion and even abhorrence of the socially accepted ideals of health and the ways of gaining it.

These patients with their resistance to healing virtually compelled the therapist to abandon his concentration on the removal of symptoms and on the return and readjustment of the patient to his environment. In this situation Freud was led step by step into a direct confrontation with the world of social relations. The farther the process of recovery advanced, the more it involved the problem of the care or neglect of the basic associations of human life.[22] Freud traced to the world of reception of early childhood the happenings and nonhappenings which cause the most serious injury to human growth.

Although Freud's thinking has some strong individualistic traits, his basic insights indicate that development into an individual is determined by the fostering of the basic associations of life. Freud sees that the ground on which one grows into a human being is the family nexus, the triad of mother-father-child (the Oedipus complex). His thinking and his lifework place the child, slighted by industrialized society, into the focus of thought and action. Thus our time has come to be characterized not only as the age of anthropology but also as the century of the child. The therapeutic movement led by Freud creates connections with childhood, the ground of life's growth, the area from which man is estranged by his preoccupation with the effort to grasp and control reality in the framework of an industrial society. Thus the long and confusing period of childhood which Descartes deplored and which he sought to escape by a firm hold on the rational elements of reality has come into view as an area rich in potentialities.

Our study of a critical phase of the Reformation to illustrate the motive power behind the discussion of the divine-human encounter indicated the central importance of whether the child and childhood appear in the focus of this discussion or disappear from it. The child disappears when the basic situation of being human is defined as a discipleship of reality, in which man through the study of nature learns to know himself, his fellowmen, and the divine. Then the long period of childhood which distinguishes man from other creatures is regarded either as merely a preparatory stage that creates the conditions for learning or else as a cumbersome obstacle to the achievement of objectivity. Such is not the case in the world of religion. While confronting the divine and speaking about the divine are understood in different ways in the various religions, somehow they always are seen to originate in the world of childhood. The experience of the presence of the divine concealed in life may be described in terms of the dependence which the child feels deeply. In reaching for the mother's breast and in looking into the mother's smiling face the child has his first experience of the faith, hope, and love which undergird life. At times the long period of childhood is described as an experience of the insecurity out of which religion grows. It is also possible to say that the "liturgy" of life takes shape when the child steps out of the world of anonymity and begins to experience life in an I-thou relation. In the "thou" of another person he confronts the mystery of the divine "Thou." The confrontation with the divine is not a matter of knowing what objective reality is; but coming to know another human being and coming to know the divine are inextricably intertwined.

In the perspective of viewing man as primarily a disciple of reality, both childhood and discourse about life as a divine-human encounter are stages of reality which a man seeking objectivity gradually leaves behind him. A classical expression of this thought is found in Auguste Comte's portrayal of human progress as a transition from the stage dominated by religion to the stage of metaphysics and finally to the stage of critical objectivity.[23] In such a formulation religion and theology must either be relegated along with man's long childhood into the world preceding the stage of critical objectivity, or else they must prove that they represent objective reality. Theology has often chosen the latter alternative.

Addressed by Life and Speaking about Life

During the academic year 1966/67 the writer had the opportunity to conduct in his university, in cooperation with the head of the department of psychology, an interdisciplinary seminar in which comparison was made between the methods of theological anthropology and of psychology in their study of man, especially their interpretations of the relation between man and nature.[24] The discussions in this seminar provide a concrete example of the situation which results from bringing theological anthropology into dialogue with a strictly empirical approach to the study of man. On the basis of the seminar and the material with which it dealt, we present the following sketch of this discussion as it brought to light the approach of "positivism of science"(A) and the approach of "positivism of revelation" (B).

A: It must be made clear from the beginning that empirical research is not interested in the content of theological concepts of man. Psychology is empirical study of human behavior. The psychologist asks: What factors lead a man to religion and theological speculation, and what factors cause society to sustain such behavior?

B: From one point of view a theologian can accept this. Psychology and theology study two different realities. When Karl

Barth,[25] the leading Protestant theologian of our time, took part in a theological conference dealing with religious experience from both a theological and a psychological point of view, he asked the chairman for permission to put a question to a lecturer who had just begun his presentation. When the permission was granted, Barth asked: Is the speaker presenting Christian theology or the psychology of religious experience? If the presentation deals with the psychology of religion, he continued, there is no reason for theologians to stay and hear it. In a theological view of man the Word of God must be the starting point of all research. Theology studies what divine revelation speaks to man.

A: The preceding statement reveals clearly how the work of the theologians appears to empirical research. In fact this seminar could well be concluded here. Perhaps there is reason, however, to continue this discussion, for on the one hand much philosophizing on man, having the nature of theological speculation, has crept into empirical research, and on the other hand there are theologians who either try to prove that their view of man is in accord with psychological research or else seek to replace an empirical psychology with a theological one. From the standpoint of empirical research it is difficult to understand why theology should seek to participate in a discussion based on a study of the facts of experience. Is not theology in a strange environment in a university, where research and learning are founded on scientific method?

B: To theology too it is important to keep clear the boundary between an empirical and a theological study of man. The interaction between them can be fruitful only if each is strictly faithful to its own method and data. It is true that an existentialist type of thinking has given rise in philosophy, psychiatry, psychotherapy, and clinical psychology to a kind of speculative study of man which neither theology nor empirical psychology can accept as such into its research. Although these approaches may contain some important insights, as a whole they are so undisciplined in method and so arbitrary in their intrusion into both psychology and theology that a definite clearing of the field is necessary. It is also true that there are theologians who have abandoned divine revelation as the basis of theological study. The interest of these theologians in the empirical sciences is an expression of their disloyalty to the method and data of theology. In extreme cases these modern theologians attempt to offer as divine revelation some views which their colleagues in philosophy, psychology, sociology, history, and other fields have already presented in their own language. Thus these theologians posing as modern are usually many steps behind the prophets of our time.[26] From the standpoint of theology the rejection by empirical research of this erroneous theological effort is to be greeted with joy.

As to the place of theological study in an academic environment, first of all the allegation that theology is speculative by nature must be completely denied. The divine revelation which it studies has been given through the mediation of history. Critical historical study of the Bible has shown that theology operates on firm historical ground. Systematic theological research, for its part, has shown that while divine revelation transcends human reason and experience, it is not contrary to them. God's eternal law makes clear the law-abiding character of nature and discloses supernatural reality to man. Thus theology may lead empirical research to find its place in the whole of reality. Psychology, for example, must admit that man has needs and goals that animals do not have.

A: Here again our paths diverge sharply. In the study of reality empirical research rejects completely the appeal to the supernatural. Man must be studied as a particular instance of the general uniformity of nature. We learn to understand the riddle of man by observing the law-abiding character of nature as a whole. What gives the whole its conformity to law gives it also to man. For this reason the experiments made on animals have decisive importance in the study of human behavior. Man is in many respects the same kind of "bundle of nerves" as the animal, a being in which the law of cause and effect, stimulus and response, is unconditioned. Man has everything that the animal has. He is a human animal.[27] This does not mean that there are no significant differences in the behavior of man and the animal. But research must hold firmly the position that the nature of man contains no elements that cannot be systematically studied and measured. In analyzing human behavior it is unnecessary to refer to supernatural or nonnatural factors. There is indeed no proof of the existence of such factors.

B: Admittedly much human behavior is determined in the same way as that of the animal kingdom. What differentiates between man and the animal, however, is that man lives by the word and that the word lives in him. By means of word and language man shares in realities from which the animal kingdom is excluded. As a being who lives in the word and by the word man has spiritual aspirations and goals alongside his biological needs and ends. These cannot be understood if man is viewed only as the highest animal. The purpose of human life cannot be derived from man's animal nature. Man's true nature becomes clear only by studying the divine word which makes man human. This divine word in all its clarity has been given to men in the divine revelation of which the Holy Scriptures speak. Only this revelation can lead a man to know who he is.

A: Human language and word-formation do not in principle distinguish man from animal. This can be explained in the same framework of conformity to law as the rest of human behavior. By trial and error, conditions are established in the child for responding to specific acts, feelings, and objects in such a way as to enable him to arrive gradually at a correct symbolic identification. Systems of reward and punishment in the family and in larger social groups reinforce in the child the proper way of responding with words to the stimuli of each situation. The ability to use language and symbols is based on the special capabilities of the human brain to develop systems of life more intricate and complex than those of animals. Even the highest achievements of the human spirit, however, grow out of man's animal nature. Man's uniqueness consists in the fact that he has learned to embody the deepest teleological purpose of nature, the incorporation of individuals into one another. This incorporation takes place first in various forms of bodily union, later by means of common language and common cultural symbols and institutional structures.

B: To this one can reply only that life is not worth living if man is this kind of slave of circumstances. It belongs to the nobility of being man to be free to choose between good and evil. The determinism of nature is broken by the fact that God has determined man to be seeker of higher ends than nature contains. In facing these ends man is a responsible being.

A: From the standpoint of empirical research these higher ends of which theologians speak may be explained in the framework of the total mechanism of human behavior. In religious expressions man defends his existence with the same mechanisms which he uses in other sectors of his life. In this perspective religion may be examined productively as a social phenomenon. Just as an individual has mechanisms with which he defends himself, so society too has defense mechanisms for protecting its basic views and beliefs. Religions are not so much explanations of the universe and reality as projective assertions about men, collectively and individually. Religion is in a sense a kind of moral geometry for finding the way in the jungle of social reality. Every group develops ideas about what is healthy and what is sick, what heals and what injures. The group presents this mental hygiene systematically in its religious institutions. The medieval church with its systems of rewards and punishments is an example of this conditioning and regulating of human life by religious beliefs.

This is only an example of the fact that supernatural reasons are unnecessary for the explanation of religious behavior. Empirical sciences must also adhere to the position that the criterion of reality is its measurability. Experimental research has demonstrated that the basic structure of being human is in learning to measure reality correctly. Growth into humanness takes place in learning what is valid and objectively verifiable experience, what can be controlled by exact comparison of various factors and components, what can be correctly seen, computed, regulated, and observed. It is therefore proper that such a measurer of life himself be examined in terms of measurement. To the degree in which man can be measured he is also understood.

B: No one will deny that there is much in man that is measurable. Yet it is precisely what is immeasurable in man that is most human. Experimental psychology has its place in explaining the mechanistic behavior that takes place in terms of man's biological needs and objectives. But psychology does not touch at all what is most deeply human, man's psychic and spiritual needs and goals. These questions dealing with the purpose of human life and man's salvation belong to the sphere of theology. Psychology can study man only from a purely human point of view, using man as the measure of all things. Theology, on the other hand, studies man in the perspective in which divine revelation places him. Here man is under divine measurement. The task of psychology is limited to the area of the natural order. It studies what shape human behavior assumes when it follows only natural instincts and seeks only natural goals. Theology, for its part, examines man as a being who seeks to satisfy psychic and spiritual needs and reaches for supernatural reality and salvation.

The summary of the seminar discussion attested the structural similarity of the two approaches. For example, the principle "what is objectively verifiable is real" is determinative for both in the same way. Scientific positivism manifests this principle in speaking about objectively verifiable facts. The positivism of revelation regards a given divine revelation as objective reality. Both refer to a specific body of data which supplies the perspective and the standard for the study. Man is defined in both cases in accordance with what is selected as most real. The difference between them is that different sets of facts are selected as the standard of evaluation in the attempt to explain what is most genuine reality.

It is also characteristic of both to interpret reality within the framework of a specific conformity to law. When the positivism of science seeks to show that man's behavior occurs in a mechanistic way, it is not content merely with setting forth this datum but makes a law out of the observation. The positivism of revelation does the same within its supernatural system. Free will and moral responsibility become a law that is applied to all men. When the divine is understood as a reality which shatters psychological determinism and gives man a free will, the nature of the divine is defined in the spirit of determinism. God is conceived as a being who regulates and conditions man anew. Just as psychological determinism makes development into humanness depend on how man learns to react to the stimuli of reality, so theological determinism sees human existence as dependent on how man reacts to the conditions which divine revelation places before him.

The seminar concentrated finally on an analysis of the thought of Michael Polanyi,[28] Hungarian-English natural scientist and philosopher. His book *Personal Knowledge*, which outlines the nature of postcritical thinking, is particularly suggestive in pointing the way out of the impasse described above. This study presents views which are in many respects quite similar to those of Luther in his controversy with Erasmus. It sheds light especially on the problem of certainty and uncertainty which loomed large in this controversy. According to Polanyi, one of the greatest threats to the progress of our culture is modern man's inability to have convictions and to express them.

In describing the process whereby personal convictions have gradually crumbled, Polanyi affirms that in European cultural development the hierarchical structure of society remained dominant for the first two thousand years in spite of many penetrating reform movements. It was not until the American and the French revolutions that this static structure was shaken. Only after these upheavals did the conviction begin to grow that the power behind the structuring of society must be the political will of the people and that men must therefore be free both in theory and in practice. Following these revolutions there have been attempts to change the system of hierarchical life and thought in two ways. One has the nature of revolution, the other that of reform. The former leads to a totalitarianism which subordinates all thinking to serve the progress and welfare of the group. The effort is to transform all of society and all thought within it in such a way as to serve the purposes of social revolution. The latter seeks to build society on the basis of the free and independent thought and action of individuals. Here the emphasis is on man's right to realize himself as radically as in the revolutionary thinking. The intellectual motivation of the social structuring based on the freedom of the individual, as in the revolutionary movements, is the defense of the freedom of men and of thought against the static authoritarianism of the hierarchical system.

While the reform movements champion the freedom of the individual, they tend to drift into the same kind of totalitarianism and absolutizing of a specific ideology as the revolutionary movements. In seeking to break free from the hierarchical structure and the authoritarian faith undergirding it, the reform movements gradually develop a mechanistic view of man which leads to a denial of man's capacity for creative thought. Personal thinking is banned as subjectivistic and arbitrary. The objective is identified with the impersonal. When this objectivism rises into power in the life of society, it means suppression of that very freedom which originally gave rise to the striving for objectivity.

In describing the character of the static hierarchical form of life, Polanyi says that it respects the basic texts of law and religion as expressions of divine authority, as divine revelation. When this static structure of social life breaks down, the supernatural authority of laws, churches, and sacred writings also breaks down. Under these conditions men build above them the authority of experience and reason in order to avoid the perils of arbitrary subjectivism. In many cases this authority becomes at least as binding as the "orthodox" authorities of the hierarchical system of life. When scientism is elevated into authority, it shackles thinking as cruelly as the medieval church ever did. Polanyi writes, "When I gave this book the sub-title 'Towards a Post-Critical Philosophy' I had this turning point in mind. The critical movement, which seems to be nearing the end of its course today, was perhaps the most fruitful effort ever sustained by the human mind. The past four or five centuries, which have gradually destroyed or overshadowed the whole medieval cosmos, have enriched us mentally and morally to an extent unrivalled by any period of similar duration." But now, he continues, we are in a situation in which we must find a new balance of our cognitive powers. We must learn to recognize that the faith out of which our life grows is the source of all conscious thinking. Following is a sketch of how this thesis is to be understood on the basis of Polanyi's research and the content of the present study.

It is fundamentally important to distinguish between subjectivistic and personal knowledge. The view which examines man as primarily a disciple of reality leads inevitably to the antitheses of subjectivism and objectivism. It labels man's subjective impressions of reality as arbitrary and misleading beliefs, and regards as most reliable the knowledge obtained when man's thinking conforms to the laws of reality. Subjective certainty and personal convictions are thus a most dangerous obstacle to obtaining contact with the truth contained in reality. The only truly dependable knowledge is that which can be proved to be universally valid. Thus faith decreases in proportion to the growth of knowledge. Polanyi describes this by referring to Locke's criticism of knowledge based on divine revelation. Locke notes that revelation cannot give certain knowledge but only leads to believing. Belief is here understood, according to Polanyi, as acceptance of subjective and personal experience which belongs to a lower order than the kind of experience and knowledge which can be objectively verified and demonstrated. If faith and divine reality are still to be valued, it is in the same sense that parliamentary democracy honors royalty on ceremonial occasions. All true power has been transferred to the "lower house" where discussion takes place in terms of objectively demonstrable propositions. Thus the human mind rejects its other cognitive capability, personal knowledge, and endeavors to build everything on the basis of a single capability. Faith is labeled as subjectivism, and all personal knowledge as an obstacle to the achievement of objectivity.

When man's immediate personal experience and knowledge are branded as arbitrary, it means that the basic associations of humanness are cut off from the soil in which humanness grows. Man's contact with the ground of life takes place primarily in terms of the kind of thinking and knowing which is not expressible in concepts. Without the aid of conceptual expressions man sees, hears, feels, and examines his environment and finds his way in it in much the same way as the animals. Man has many thoughts which are not derived from knowledge mediated by language. Human action depends in large measure upon this inarticulate and unconceptualized knowledge. In portraying the relation of this unconceptualized knowledge to conceptualized knowledge, Polanyi affirms that this unconscious and tacit knowing and experiencing exerts decisive influence upon all conscious thought. This is not merely a matter of subjective feeling; it is the same kind of effort to obtain objective knowledge of reality, independent of the individual experience of the subject, as conceptual knowledge represents. This personal component is by no means an obstacle to conscious knowledge. On the contrary, it is the compass needle of conscious knowledge in the search for contact with reality. The human person shapes knowledge both on the lower stages and in the highest achievements of the human intellect.

Polanyi describes the difference between unexpressed and expressed knowledge by comparing the behavior of rats and men. Investigators of the behavior of rats have demonstrated that rats find their way out of a maze in ways that indicate an inner construction of a map of the labyrinth. Man's behavior has the same basic structure, but man has the advantage of being able to make an explicit map or to have one made. To find the way by means of a ready-made map is easier than to search without such a map. The use of a map, however, contains the danger that it may be misleading. A critical examination of the map thus becomes necessary. The map may be examined and made more accurate by comparing it with the terrain which it represents. Thus the peril of the unreliability of conceptually expressed knowledge is lessened, for it is possible to examine it critically. The map may be studied as an objective reality outside ourselves. As such it can speak to us, and it does speak regardless of whether we ourselves have made it or not. If we ourselves have made it, in examining it we are listening critically to what we have previously said.

Such critical examination is impossible at the stage where knowledge is inarticulate. A chart that is only in our mind can be tested and rectified only by using it as a guide. If we go astray, we can correct it. Inarticulate knowledge cannot be revised in any other way. It is not critical in the same way as expressed knowledge. It is like a small lighted area in the midst of immeasurable darkness, a narrow path illumined by precritical instinctive wisdom. Conceptual knowledge, on the other hand, affords a panoramic view of the whole universe and grows under the control of critical examination.

How can this inarticulate human knowledge, man's personal participation in the shaping of conscious thought, govern all human thinking? Do not these examples indicate, to the contrary, the wisdom of giving priority to those human capabilities which enable man to overcome preverbal dumbness and to achieve accurate logical knowledge? Must not the ideal be the kind of learning from reality in which the influence of man's personal contribution and of his inarticulate experience decreases? To this Polanyi replies: To be sure, a traveler proceeding with the aid of a map is in an intellectually more advantageous position than an explorer of a new area who lacks a map. Yet the progress which the explorer makes with his groping is a higher human achievement than a well-planned tourist trip by the traveler with a map. The attainment of knowledge as exact as possible is an important human objective, but man's finest intellectual achievement is the creation of knowledge. The human mind is most sensitive as it brings uncharted areas under its control. It is then that man renews his articulate knowledge, the framework on which he depends in his search for knowledge. The genuinely new can be found only by means of the same inarticulable powers which the animals use in learning to find their way out of mazes. What differentiates man from animal is not primarily the capacity for verbal expression but the inarticulable properties of thought and experience upon which verbal language depends.

In a sense the learning of language involves the same process as the application of scientific theory. As man learns to use language he shares in the fashioning of a universal theory about reality. In speaking about things he tests his theory. So long as language classifies things well, man is satisfied with it and accepts the implied theory. The application of language to things is inarticulate. Man's personal participation in speech is such that his unverbalized and unspoken knowledge and thought ("Ineffable Domain") play a decisive role. This is the case no matter how rich a language becomes.

The development of language to represent reality has also another fundamental limitation. Just as a map representing an area in its natural size is unnecessary and unusable, such is also the case with language striving for this kind of exactness. Language can be an aid to thinking, according to Polanyi, only if its symbols can be organized ever anew in such a way that their use is easier than that of the things which they represent. Man's rational superiority over the animals is based chiefly on his ability to make such use of the symbols representing experience as to keep his experience open to new information. This capacity for reinterpreting experience depends mainly on inarticulate powers. The interaction between the inarticulate and the articulate, unverbalized and verbalized thought and knowledge, is crucially important for growth into humanness. On the one hand man's silent capacities grow as articulation develops. On the other hand inarticulate thinking prevents conscious thought from becoming petrified. Articulate speech can hinder the activity of ineffable thought. In order to portray reality in the richest possible way language must become less exact. As the exactness of language decreases, the inarticulate powers have more play. Thus man's personal participation in speech, the way in which he experiences the tension between his unspoken thoughts and his symbolic operations, makes human experience poor or rich.

Polanyi's theory of the nature of thought and language is in sharp contradiction to the method of interpretation born in the spirit of Descartes and expressed by Wittgenstein in his early years in the form of an aphorism, "Of what cannot be said thereof one must be silent." To this Polanyi replies, "Nothing that we know can be said precisely." Words as such have no significance. Only a speaking or listening man can give them any meaning. Words and thoughts are always attached to a network of words and thoughts belonging to a specific human group. In this network man finds his problems and seeks solutions to them. In no situation can a man say anything with complete exactness. Words obtain in each case the meaning which the speaker gives to them. Usually a man does not know exactly what he means by his words each time. In examining what he means he becomes convinced that words signify more than he consciously knows, if they are to carry any meaning at all.

In a sense man both begets his thoughts and is begotten by them. By creating symbolic forms man gives birth and lasting existence to thought. But these symbolic constructs also have the power to control man's thinking. They speak to him and convince him. Polanyi asks: What must we do in this situation? How are we to escape the alternatives of dogmatism and positivism? To the question, "Who convinces whom?" there is a simple answer, "I seek to convince myself." A man must learn to let his own judgment determine the evaluation of all intellectual achievements.

To cast personal knowledge and thought aside and to fail to give them attention, according to Polanyi, creates a dangerous vacuum which the languages of various power groups seek to fill. When the effort is made to build a life together according to the ideal of an objective impersonal knowledge which excludes a large area of the human person, the inevitable result is a collectivism that stifles human existence. The material welfare of the group becomes the main objective, and scientific thinking is harnessed to serve the development of the community into a welfare state.

Polanyi sees this development as a threat to the spirit which impels scientific work. Research is no longer guided by the human quest but by supraindividual forces. Creative scientific study, however, demands the spirit of inquiry which is characteristic of inarticulate thinking. This thinking is organically related to man's growth and change. Upon finding a solution, man is on the move toward a new problem. Having made a discovery, he does not view himself or the world as he did before. His vision has changed, and he has made of himself a new person who sees and thinks in a different way. In bridging the gap between the problem and its solution man changes along with the framework in which he has interpreted reality. A discovery is always creative. As man discovers, his personality changes. Thus creative thinking is possible only in a spirit of daring and in a "heuristic passion" for discovery. If man refuses to grow and evades change, his thinking becomes schematized. Unwillingness to change leads man to do violence to facts. To regard objective impersonal knowledge as the highest ideal has the tragic consequence of quenching the spirit of inquiry which issues from the depths of existence. According to Polanyi, positivistic empiricism is only superficially experiential and contains a large measure of violence toward the world of human experience.

Theology within the Exploration of Life

In the light of Polanyi's analysis of the structure of the "positivism of science" we see also the destructive effects of the "positivism of revelation" upon man's being and upon the unity of human life. A positivism of revelation which interprets Christianity as absolute objective truth has brought about conceptual and social structuring which has fragmented the basic unity of the fabric of human life. Representing this fragmentation are the antitheses to which the present study has referred: divine revelation–human reason, theocentric–anthropocentric, supernatural–natural, the church–the world, Christendom–the pagan world. This approach is as high-handed in dealing with human experience as is scientific positivism, for it stifles the basic language of life, the word of life upon which growth into humanness depends.

The ultimate purpose of our study has been to bring into the focus of anthropological research the language of life which issues from man's long childhood. The human experience which is the object of theological study is concerned with the cultivation of this basic language. All quest for encounter with the divine is in some form or other an endeavor to live and abide in this word of life, listening to its speech and seeking contact with the speaker. The essential nature of all striving for a confrontation with the divine resembles the way in which a child lives and moves in the world where he is received. As theology concentrates on the analysis and description of this confrontation, it must join other anthropological research in supplementing the method of conceptual analysis, now dominant in theology, with other methods. This is necessary if it is to transmit to the study of man the message of the basic language of life. Protestant theological anthropology in particular has become estranged from an analysis of the problem of the fundamental situation of being human and of the language which life itself speaks. It has become predominantly a revelation-centered and church-centered theology which conceives the confrontation between the divine and the human as taking place primarily by means of the history recorded in the Scriptures or by means of the church. Thus the encounter with the divine is regarded as a situation in which man listens to the proclamation transmitting the message of the biblical texts or else as one in which man determines his relation to the divine by his relation to the church and its means of grace. In the former case, theology concentrates almost convulsively upon the effort to demonstrate that divine revelation is given by means of history and upon the hermeneutical problems dealing with the interpretation of the texts given in history. Theological research has been driven to this position by the necessity of having to defend itself against the criticism it has met from the positivistic views described above. By emphasizing the historicity of revelation it attempts to demonstrate the objective character of the divine words and acts. Theology thus becomes a defense of the interpretation of a specific area of reality. In the latter case, theology assumes a similar apologetic character, but here what is defended is not a doctrine or an interpretation but an ecclesiastical structure. Theology becomes a denominational ideology by which a church body rationalizes its existence and defends its right to be a separate entity. Theological study in this case is focused upon an analysis of the nature of the church and its means of grace.

We have sketched in bold relief, approaching a caricature, the tendencies which lead to a setting up of the divine and the human as opposites and have sought to trace this antithesis to its original sources. This presentation shows the one-sidedness of the participation of Protestant theology in the research on the basic meaning of humanness. The present study itself with its method of conceptual analysis is a telling example of the situation. It indicates above all the limitations of this type of study. It is apparent that outside of theological study, rather than in theology itself, one finds more of the kind of "theological" elucidation of the nature of divine humanness, of the basic associations of life and their fragmentation, where conceptual analysis is not predominant but where methods are shaped by a concrete encounter with man.

A theology which concentrates primarily on conceptual analysis has only remote contact with the dynamics of personal experience and thought. This is illustrated by the fact that Protestant theological education, for the most part, is training solely for conceptual analysis and verbal communication. There is an obvious discrepancy between academic learning and clinical experience.[29] Yet in the work of a minister, as in that of a physician, jurist, engineer, teacher, industrial manager, or military officer, what is primarily needed is skill and inarticulate wisdom rather than conscious application of theory. In speaking about the threat which the positivistic view of science imposes on the most sensitive aspects of the scientific heritage, Polanyi[30] points out that science operates by the scientist's own skill and ability. The scientist's personal participation is a significant factor in even the most exact operations. No phenomenon, for example, unconditionally refutes alleged probabilities. The scientist must decide personally what he considers to be too improbable. The ends of proficient accomplishment are achieved by conforming to rules which the person obeying them does not know as such, as in the case of skill in riding a bicycle. Skill of this type cannot be transferred from one person to another by description, for the skill cannot be described. The master must set the example which the apprentice follows. The apprentice pays attention to the master, for he has confidence[31] in his way of doing things, although the master cannot explain in detail the grounds of his proficiency. The apprentice learns his master's skill in a partly subconscious way, and he learns something which the master does not know in a way which he can describe. The articulate content of science can easily be transferred from one culture to another and from

one geographical area to another, but such is not the case with
the indefinable skill of scientific research. If a generation fails
to cultivate such skill, it is lost for future practice. If society
wants to preserve personal knowledge and thought, it must learn
to respect this heritage by keeping in close personal contact with
the masters of each area of life.

In the study of the experience of confrontation with the
divine, the positivism of revelation and church-centered theology
have exerted the same kind of influence as the positivism of science in the general area of scientific research. When, for example, the organizing principle of theological thought is the idea
that divine revelation is given by means of history,[32] the result is
a disregard for the personal and direct encounter with the divine,
which is implied in the sacred writings constituting the main
source of Christian theology. The same is true of the study of
the history of the Christian churches. It becomes primarily a
history of ideas and dogmas, not of persons. From the sacred
writings a history of redemption is singled out, and from the
common history of mankind a special history of the church is set
forth. History of this type is connected by very thin threads with
the fundamental human experience of the divine, which has given
birth both to the sacred writings and to church history. The positivism of revelation emphasizes the transmission of the divine
word from one human group to another and from one generation to another by means of historical documents, and posits the
proclamation and hearing of this historically grounded word as
the condition for the encounter with the divine. In so doing it
damages the sensitive inner core of personal encounter with the
divine, which has a tradition and succession of its own. When
divine revelation is regarded as confronting man chiefly by means
of a verbal proclamation of the sacred writings, doubt is cast
upon that heritage and succession of divine confrontation which
is experienced in the preverbal world of the basic language of
life and in the basic associations from which life grows.

The positivism of revelation here reveals its bondage to the
idealistic conception of the nature of language and word. It is
interesting to observe that in the world of Greek culture "lan-

guage" was no problem at all. The Greek language contains no word that is the equivalent of the concept of language as it is used in present linguistic research.[33] The fundamental expression is the word *logos*, which contains the implication that man with his language names reality. When man is thus viewed as primarily a being who is seeking by means of his language to give right names to reality, as a disciple of reality, then the human use of language is seen only as a conscious act. To the Greeks it was self-evident that their language was the only true human language and that all other languages were barbaric.

When western Christendom searches for the basic human language of life, it enters into a relationship with the idealism which has its roots in Greek culture. This is evident already in the New Testament, a book written in Greek. A task of gigantic difficulty confronts the writers of the New Testament as they seek to express in Greek their inquiries into the mystery of the Trinity and the incarnation, the secret content of the basic language of human life. Although they use the most ordinary everyday language, they also take the most highly developed terms of the Greek language, such as *logos*, to express their experience of the manifestation of life and the hearing of the word of life. Ever since New Testament times Christendom has been engaged in the twofold process of blending together the Judeo-Christian and the classical Greek heritages and of differentiating between them, as was indicated by the discussion between Luther and Erasmus. In the light of this discussion one of the principal tasks of theology becomes the study of the nature of the fundamental inarticulate language of life.

Church-centered theology is structurally similar in many respects to the positivism of revelation. Yet it seeks to absolutize not a language but a "church." A social form of life is understood to represent divine revelation. In taking for granted that the community represents objective reality it resembles the idealistic conception of the relation between society and the individual. Just as the positivism of revelation refutes the pathology of language, so church-centered thinking evades the pathology of society and its institutions.

The writer obtained a concrete experience of this in a theological conference in 1964 which dealt with the relation between Christianity and Judaism.[34] Its general theme was "The Church and the Jews." When the discussion centered on the persecution of the Jews, so dreadfully manifest in the history of the Christian churches, and the mass annihilation of the Jews, carried out by our own generation in the midst of Christendom, one would have expected the pathology of church communities to come into the focus of attention. Yet the discussion tended to steer away again and again from coming to grips with the violence which men collectively perpetrate on their fellowmen. It remained instead on the level of explaining the biblical view of the church and its bearing upon the relation between the Christian church and Judaism. A rabbi representing Judaism expressed repeatedly his bewilderment over the way in which theologians speak about the church: in speaking about the Jews they speak about people, but in referring to Christendom they use the term *church*. They admit that individual Christians may have strayed into acts of violence, but in the same breath they declare that the church has always promoted love and righteousness and opposed all persecution. Jews are considered to be people who have taken the position of opposing divine election and revelation, while Christians are the church which represents this revelation. The Jewish people and even the Jew are confronted not by Christian men but by the church. The message of the violence in the common history of Jews and Christians is thus shunted off from consciousness and covered up with discussion of the principles of the church in dealing with the Jewish question.

One of the most fateful items in the present theological vocabulary is *Church*, spelled with a capital C. In its effort to define the biblical or New Testament view of the church, the theology of our time, grandiloquently called the "Century of the Church," has discovered that the Scriptures offer insuperable resistance[35] to the bombastic tendency. Yet this concept has stubbornly remained in the center of both professionally theological and ecumenical conversation. From the viewpoint of the theme of the present study it is especially tragic to absolutize the churches by viewing the church as the instrument of divine election and revelation. Luther's theology and particularly his book *The Bondage of the Will* showed that this way of thinking and the social structuring based upon it stand in the way of the confrontation between the human and the divine. Luther issued the call to a life-centered theology, away from a revelation-centered and a church-centered theology. The research which serves the basic language of life and the growth of divine humanness must do more than afford training for discipleship of reality. It must learn to share in that creative work of the giver of life which gives birth to a new humanity in the midst of the old.

Notes and References
Bibliography
Index

Notes and References

The translations from the Weimarer Ausgabe (Weimar, 1883–) are those of the translator. Corresponding references, where they exist, are cited by volume and page in the American Edition of Luther's Works (Philadelphia: Fortress; and Saint Louis: Concordia, 1955–). Full facts of publication for other references are found in the bibliography.

1. Man the Explorer

1. "Scientists—that is, creative scientists—spend their lives trying to guess right. They are sustained and guided therein by their heuristic passion. . . . Major discoveries change our interpretative framework. Hence it is logically impossible to arrive at these by the continuous application of our previous interpretative framework" (Michael Polanyi, *Personal Knowledge*, p. 143). "Scientific discovery reveals new knowledge, but the new vision which accompanies it is not knowledge. It is less than knowledge, for it is a guess; but it is more than knowledge, for it is a foreknowledge of things yet unknown and at the present perhaps inconceivable" (ibid., p. 135; cf. Karl R. Popper, *The Logic of Scientific Discovery*).

2. Cf. Anders Nygren's discussion of the objectivity of theology, *Filosofi och motivforskning*, pp. 168–86. See Aarne Siirala, "Lundilaisen teologian käsitys systemaattisen teologian tehtävästä."

3. Joseph Haroutunian describes church-centered theology of revelation as follows: "Theology in the Western churches has been at the service of the organized churches as the means of grace, and this fact has been a primary factor in the making of the theologies in our historical background. There is no doctrine in orthodox Christian theology that is not in line with the purposes and interests of the ecclesiastical establishments called churches" (*God with Us: A Theology of Transpersonal Life*, pp. 279–83). For a description of other types, see Paul Tillich, *The Future of Religions*, pp. 91–93.

4. The final two sections in the third chapter of this study develop further the themes here presented.

5. Cf. Michael Polanyi, *Personal Knowledge*, pp. 142–45, 150–60; idem, *The Study of Man*.

6. Tillich (*Future of Religions*, pp. 80–94), in the last lecture of his life, deals with the significance of the history of religions for systematic theology. Here he refutes both the view that only the theologian's own religion deserves to be called true religion (*vera religio*) while other religions are only gropings toward the divine (*religiones falsae*), and the attempt to create a radically secular theology which does not need the concept *God*. "In order to reject both this old and new orthodox attitude, one must accept the following systematic presuppositions. First, one must say that revelatory experiences are universally human. Religions are based on something that is given to a man wherever he lives. . . . There are revealing and saving powers in all religions. . . . The second assumption states that revelation is received by man in terms of his finite human situation. . . . It is received always in a distorted form . . . " (ibid., p. 81). Tillich presents two other presuppositions which do not concern the present study.

2. *A Phase of an Eternal Quest*

1. For the presentation of Luther in the general history of philosophy, see Brian A. Gerrish, *Grace and Reason*, p. 4; for the Roman Catholic interpretations, see Bernhard Lohse, *Ratio und Fides*, pp. 7–81; for Melanchthon's attitude toward the issue in question, see Andreas Flitner, *Erasmus im Urteil seiner Nachwelt*, pp. 14–17.

2. Werner Jaeger (*Humanism and Theology*, pp. 13, 65) describes Erasmus as a pioneer of Christian humanism and Luther as an antihumanist who ridiculed the pagan Aristotle.

3. For Bertrand Russell's evaluation of Erasmus and of Luther, see *A History of Western Philosophy*, p. 450.

4. Jacques Maritain (*Three Reformers: Luther, Descartes, Rousseau*, p. 6) says that Luther replaced God and Christ with the human ego as the main object of theological study. He bases his argument principally on the researches of Heinrich Denifle (*Luther und Luthertum in der ersten Entwicklung*) and Hartmann Grisar (*Luther*). Maritain portrays Luther as an antiintellectualist (*Three Reformers*, p. 30).

5. Ragnar Bring points out that Erasmus was actually closer to the Augustinian position than to the Pelagian ("Kring uppgörelsen mellan

Erasmus och Luther," pp. 170–226, 238–44). Harry J. McSorley (*Luther: Right or Wrong?*) claims that Erasmus's approach was a reflection of the theological unclarity of the late Middle Ages (ibid., p. 279). Luther was first influenced by the neo-semi-Pelagianism of the late Scholasticism (Biel, Ockham; ibid., pp. 191–224). Through Augustine Luther then discovered the biblical and catholic doctrine of "grace alone" (ibid., pp. 227 ff., 353 ff.).

6. Ernst Wilhelm Kohls claims that Erasmus was a Christ-centered biblical theologian. The differences between Luther and Erasmus were only in the different emphases in their interpretation of Scripture (*Die Theologie des Erasmus*, 1:175–80).

7. Orval Hobart Mowrer, *The New Group Therapy*, pp. 3–8.

8. Sigmund Freud, *Autobiography*, p. 27.

9. Cf. Anders Nygren, *Agape and Eros;* Rudolf Johannesson, *Person och Gemenskap.*

10. On the background of the controversy between Erasmus and Luther, cf. Lennart Pinomaa, *Lutherin kilvoitteleva usko*, pp. 44–46.

11. *WA* 18, 786, 30.

12. Cf. Heinrich Bornkamm, *Luthers geistige Welt.*

13. On Erasmus's effort to evade conflicts, see John C. Olin, *Desiderius Erasmus: Christian Humanism and the Reformation*, p. 145; Johann Huizinga, *Erasmus and the Age of Reformation*, p. 161.

14. According to Erasmus, Luther shatters the dreams of humanism. See Erik H. Erikson, *Young Man Luther: A Study in Psychoanalysis and History*, p. 193.

15. Gerhard Ebeling on Luther's criticism of the tenor of Erasmus's style of writing: "For the right word is an event of love. Therefore God's word as authority for faith is authority for love, for God is love, and this is the source and the end of all speaking about God. Indeed, as Luther, shocked at Erasmus's frosty ice-cold way of speaking about God, says with the full assurance of ultimate wisdom, God is 'a glowing baking-oven of love' " (*Luther. Einfuhrüng in sein Denken*, p. 309). For Luther's reference in *The Bondage of the Will* to Erasmus's use of words, see *WA* 18, 611, 5. Cf. Nygren, *Agape and Eros*, pp. 576–77.

16. Erasmus understands Luther to say: man has no merits; all of man's acts, even the pious ones, are sin; man is clay in the hands of the potter. See Ernst F. Winter, *Erasmus–Luther: Discourse on Free Will*, p. 81.

17. On Luther's grappling with paternal and ecclesiastical authority, cf. Erickson, *Young Man Luther*, pp. 49–98.

18. See Winter, *Erasmus–Luther*, pp. 3–12.

19. Ibid., pp. 8–9.

20. Already in the year 1518 Luther says: *Liberum arbitrium . . . res est de solo titulo*, "as to free will, the thing is only a title" (*WA* 1, 359, 33–36 [*LW* 31, 48–49]).

21. Erasmus respected the church fathers for their learning. He was horrified by Luther's belittling of the views of others. Cf. John W. Aldridge, *The Hermeneutic of Erasmus*, p. 89. According to Aldridge, Erasmus is a humanist in quest of original sources, while Luther is a "medieval" dogmatician (ibid., p. 37). Yrjö J. E. Alanen says that Luther strayed into rationalistic determinism and in *The Bondage of the Will* remained stuck in the heritage of Scholasticism (*Valinta ja Vastuu*, p. 68). He also claims that in this work Luther abandoned his own theological foundations (ibid., p. 168).

22. Kohls (*Theologie des Erasmus*, 1:193) says that Erasmus consistently represents a living scriptural theology. He claims that Erasmus developed a purely biblical theology already before his debate with Luther. According to Kohls, when Erasmus speaks of the freedom of the will, he means the scriptural view of the human will as a will open to God's will (ibid., p. 161). Kohls says that Erasmus examines man solely from the viewpoint of the relation to God and the divine work of redemption accomplished by the cross of Christ. Erasmus's basic position is scriptural, although he supplements his view with material from the philosophy of Plato and Aristotle. According to Kohls, Erasmus regards philosophers as authoritative only when they are in accord with the Bible (ibid., p. 87). To Erasmus the Bible is the only source of revelation (ibid., pp. 126–27). In this respect Erasmus was "committed" to the Christian faith. Cf. McSorley's discussion whether Erasmus was a skeptic (*Luther*, pp. 279 ff.).

23. On Erasmus's exegetical principles, see Kohls, *Theologie des Erasmus*, 1:127–37. Aldridge (*Hermeneutic of Erasmus*, p. 97) says that Luther's dogmatic scriptural principle triumphed because the age sought faith. Men were not yet mature enough to accept the critical objectivity represented by Erasmus.

24. Cf. Winter, *Erasmus–Luther*, pp. 6, 9–10; Kohls, *Theologie des Erasmus*, 1:61. For Luther's reaction, see *WA* 18, 603, 22–29.

25. *Quid enim incertitudine miserius?* "For what is more wretched than uncertainty?" (*WA* 18, 604, 33). "But they begin to say, it may

be so, but how do we know what is the word of God, what is right or wrong? That we must learn from the pope and the councils. Let them infer and say whatever they wish, but I say: you cannot put your trust in it or quiet your conscience with it. It is your existence, your life, that is involved. God must therefore say to your heart, this is God's word, otherwise it remains undecided. . . . They present the following assertion of Saint Augustine, 'I would not have believed the gospel, did not the authority of the church compel me.' . . . But you must say, how does it concern me whether it was said by Augustine or Jerome, Saint Peter or Saint Paul, or even archangel Gabriel from heaven, which is much more? It does not help me, I must have God's word, I must know what God says to me" (*WA* 10I,2, 335, 14–27). Cf. A. E. Koskenniemi, ed., *Martti Luther. Kirkkopostilla III.*

26. *WA* 18, 604, 5.

27. Cf. Harald Ostergaard-Nielsen, *Scriptura Sacra et Viva Vox*, pp. 14–28. "Whether one recognizes Erasmus as representative of the Catholic church or not, the concept of authority is the same for Erasmus and for the Catholic church. Both stand here, together with all Protestant metaphysical theology, united against Luther in the question which was to him the decisive issue, namely, the question of the clarity or unclarity of Scripture" (ibid., p. 28).

28. Cf. Winter, *Erasmus–Luther*, pp. 9–11.

29. *WA TR* 1, 16, 13 (No. 46); (*LW* 54, 7).

30. Cf. Aarne Siirala, *Gottes Gebot bei Martin Luther*, pp. 54–105.

31. See *WA* 18, 654, 10–30.

32. According to Aland, Luther meant by the clarity of the Bible its clear answers to questions of faith: In Scripture no question of faith remains in darkness. Cf. Kurt Aland, *Kirchengeschichtliche Entwürfe*, pp. 396, 400.

33. Cf. Alanen, *Valinta ja Vastuu.*

34. For Luther's presentation of the clarity of the Bible, see *WA* 18, 606–11. As an example of the artificiality of Luther's argument, see *WA* 18, 681–99.

35. Cf. Jaroslav Pelikan, *Obedient Rebels.*

36. Karl Holl (*Luther*, 1:180) presents Luther's struggle during the years in the monastery as an effort to fulfill an unattainable ethical ideal. Cf. Aarne Siirala, "Mitä on spiritualismi?"

37. For interpretations of Luther as supplanting the authority of the church with the authority of the Bible, see John M. Todd, *Martin Luther*, pp. 282–88; and Leonard E. Elliott-Binns, *Erasmus the Reformer,* p. 41. According to Elliott-Binns, until the Leipzig debate Luther acknowledged the authority of the pope, until Worms he acknowledged the authority of the councils, after that only the authority of the Bible, still later only certain parts of the Bible, finally only the authority of his own inner self.

38. On Luther's interpretation of the first commandment, i.e., despising one's own being as violation of the first commandment, cf. A. Siirala, *Gottes Gebot*, pp. 61–88. For data on Luther's view of the Bible, see ibid., pp. 105–78.

39. Cf. Erikson's presentation of the ideological responsibility of the man of science, *Young Man Luther*, p. 20.

40. Cf. ibid., pp. 47, 198–208.

41. Cf. Winter, *Erasmus–Luther*, pp. 13–20.

42. On the significance of the year 1525 in Luther's life, cf. Paul Althaus, *Luthers Haltung im Bauernkrieg*, p. 63.

43. On Luther's inner conflicts, see Lennart Pinomaa, *Lutherin kilvoitteleva usko*, pp. 59–76; idem, ed., *Teologia etsii suuntaa*, p. 49; Horst Beintker, *Die Uberwindung der Anfechtung bei Luther*. For Luther's own expression in *The Bondage of the Will*, see *WA* 18, 719, 4.

44. On the appeal of the rebels to Luther's writings and his *sola scriptura* principle, see Althaus, *Luthers Haltung*, pp. 14–16; Pinomaa, *Lutherin kilvoitteleva usko*, p. 22.

45. On Luther's conception of authority and his explanation of the fourth commandment, cf. A. Siirala, *Gottes Gebot*, pp. 178–266. Every man must live in subordination to another. On the responsibility of parenthood, see *WA* 6, 251, 35; 6, 253, 11; 40^I, 512, 29 (*LW* 26, 332). Cf. Erikson, *Young Man Luther*, p. 66. On parenthood and government as instruments of the divine word, see *WA* 30^{II}, 55, 5–30. Cf. Werner Elert, *The Structure of Lutheranism*, p. 49; idem, *Der Christliche Glaube*, p. 111.

46. According to Luther, the task of all government and parenthood is to protect the growth of humanness; they do not represent any "order of creation": "All created orders are God's masks, allegories, by which he sets forth his theology rhetorically; they should be seen as containing Christ" (*WA* 40^I, 483, 9 [*LW* 26, 310]). "Therefore they are all

offices and fruits of the Holy Spirit: to take care of children, to love wife, to obey magistrates, these are fruits of the Spirit. Among the papists these are carnal, because they do not understand the meaning of creation" (*WA* 40^I, 348, 2 [*LW* 26, 216]). Cf. Gustav Törnvall: "The content of righteousness in *iustitia civilis* is thus nothing else than Christ's righteousness, applied to the worldly regiment" (*Andligt och världsligt regemente hos Luther*, p. 172).

47. See Martin Seils, *Der Gedanke von Zusammenwirken Gottes und des Menschen in Luthers Theologie*, pp. 170–76.

48. On Luther's reference to the central importance of *The Bondage of the Will* in his literary production, see Pinomaa, *Teologia*, p. 51.

49. See *WA* 18, 634.

50. On the nature of human willing, see *WA* 18, 635. On the primary decision as not being conscious, cf. Hans E. Hengstenberg, *Philosophische Anthropologie*.

51. Cf. Winter, *Erasmus–Luther*, pp. 69–79. Kohls (*Theologie des Erasmus*, 2:51) says that to Erasmus grace meant above all the offer of grace which affords man the possibility of deciding whether to be a soldier of Christ or a follower of the devil. Erasmus does not regard this possibility of decision as an autonomous property of man but as a situation provided for man by the fulfillment of salvation history in Christ. Kohls says that this view of Erasmus is in harmony with Thomas Aquinas's doctrine of grace. Cf. Christian Dolfen, *Die Stellung des Erasmus von Rotterdam zur scholastischen Methode*; Pinomaa, *Lutherin kilvoitteleva usko*, p. 47.

52. *WA* 18, 706.

53. On the various uses of the law in Luther's theology, see Lauri Haikola, *Gesetz und Evangelium bei Matthius Flacius Illyricus*, pp. 84–142.

54. When Luther speaks of creation as a reality reflecting the face of God and as the "mask" of God, he is criticizing the mechanistic views of reality and man represented by Scholasticism. "The whole creation is the face and mask of God" (*WA* 40^I, 174, 13 [*LW* 26, 95]). "All creatures are God's masks and disguises" (*WA* 17^{II}, 192, 28). Cf. Törnvall: "Luther opposed the scholastic conception of creation because it understood the world in an atomistic and mechanistic way" (*Andligt och världsligt*, p. 173); Wilhelm Maurer: "Thus the creative love which gave life to the whole world is also the basic cause for the mission of the Son and the rule of the Holy Spirit. God's work in nature and in the history of salvation is uni-

form, an ever repeated creation out of nothing" (*Von der Freiheit eines Christenmenschen*, p. 88). Eulalio R. Baltazar ("Teilhard de Chardin: A Philosophy of Procession," p. 13), speaks of conversion from a substantialistic to a personalistic way of thinking in Roman Catholicism. "Aristotelo-Thomism approached man wholly from the side of his nature. Man was seen as an essence or being-as-object. But such a notion does not reveal the deepest in man, his uniqueness and subjectivity. . . . The basic flaw in the scholastic solution to the problem of nature and supernature was to relate grace to nature instead of to personality" (ibid., p. 148). Cf. Pierre Teilhard de Chardin, *Man's Place in Nature*, pp. 262–64.

55. See *WA* 18, 635, 20.

56. On the commandments as exposing the basic flaws in human existence, see Paul Althaus, *The Divine Command*.

57. For the twofold character of the commandments, see *WA* 18, 695–96. Cf. Lennart Pinomaa, *Faith Victorious: An Introduction to Luther's Theology*, pp. 66–67. On Luther's interpretation of the Decalogue, see A. Siirala, *Gottes Gebot*, pp. 22–53.

58. On being elect versus self-chosen worship: "From this you see what true worship of God is. Because he has given all things, houses, wives, . . . for all these things we give him thanks. This is true worship of God. From this you understand the falsity of the Mass. Thus all the religious people sin against the first commandment" (*WA* 30[I], 3, 21–35). Cf. Gustaf Wingren, *Luther on Vocation*, p. 73; Johann Haar, *Initium Creaturae Dei*, p. 102; Törnvall, *Andligt och världsligt*, p. 145.

59. For Luther's interpretation of Abraham as elect, see *WA* 40[I], 404, 27 (*LW* 26, 257); 40[I], 405, 11 (*LW* 26, 257–58); 40[I], 406, 11 (*LW* 26, 258); 43, 229, 1–20 (*LW* 4, 130); 43, 594, 4–15 (*LW* 5, 240).

60. *WA TR* 5, 439–41 (6017). Cf. Wilhelm Link, *Das Ringen Luthers um die Freiheit der Theologie von der Philosophie*, p. 192.

61. *WA* 56, 255, 18; 56, 307, 17. Cf. Georg Wünsch, *Luther und die Gegenwart*, pp. 88, 103–9.

62. For the concept *world of reception*, see Martti Siirala: "The reception experienced by every child—his 'receiving world'—may be outlined from various angles, but one important angle is that the reception has a long historical dimension: any reception is the result of a long process, created individually and collectively. A receiving-process has an aim: living that is specifically human. This is true of every phase in the being of man, of every formative stage: heredity,

conception, pregnancy, delivery, early and later infancy, school age and pre-puberty, puberty, adolescence, adulthood, middle age, senescence, and so on—these are 'human'. All these phases are conducted in the 'atmosphere' of our preconceptions, though some are more responsibly acknowledged than others. The events are shot through with our basic views and beliefs—and also with *our* passivity. They are permeated with both our ideologies and *our* despair, *our* freedom and *our* dependence, *our* tradition and *our* chaotic 'drives'."

63. On the superiority of natural over artificial language, see *WA* 18, 80, 17 (*LW* 40, 96–97); 18, 186, 38 (*LW* 40, 197); 18, 188, 12 (*LW* 40, 198). On networks of language, see Benjamin L. Whorf, *Language, Thought and Reality*; Lancelot L. Whyte, *The Next Development in Man*; idem, *The Unconscious before Freud*.

64. God's church is where the word of life is in use: "The church encompasses within itself the God who speaks with us" (*WA* 43, 600, 10 [*LW* 5, 248]). God speaks to us in our fellowmen: "For to whom will you present your needs except to God? And where can you find him except in your brother?" (*WA* 15, 488, 30). The divine and the human are intertwined: "But he does not work in us without us, and for this purpose he creates and ministers, in order that he might operate in us and we might cooperate with him" (*WA* 18, 745, 4). God speaks and comforts in men and by means of men (*WA* 18, 754, 15).

65. On *viva vox*, see Ostergaard-Nielsen: "Bultmann's speech concerning God seems to tend toward becoming fixed on an 'anonymous God,' as also his speech concerning man moves in the direction of an 'anonymous man,' that is, it seems to point principally to a solitary man. Bultmann has not penetrated into an understanding of the Word as something which establishes community. Therefore he does not see that what is determinative is not only that 'the word is spoken' but above all who does the speaking" (*Scriptura Sacra*, pp. 61–62). "When Luther concludes that where the oral word is denied there the gospel itself is denied, the 'oral word' here is not simply identical with the 'external word.' The 'oral word' is not a mere repetition of the word of Scripture. The oral word is here the word that has a content of personal comfort and a form that is shaped by personal pronouns" (ibid., p. 208). "He who speaks in the name of Jesus speaks many a word which the historical Jesus perhaps never spoke and which therefore is not recorded in Scripture, and yet such words are 'Jesus' own words' when they are spoken in his name" (ibid., p. 214).

66. *WA* 3, 281, 1.

67. *WA* 18, 602, 30.

68. The presence of the divine is a "kingdom of hearing": "the blessings of the gospel are to be heard" (*WA* 40^I, 401, 2 [*LW* 26, 255]). Life is realized as cultivation of the word: "This light has been shining from the beginning of the world, and God's word has been preached in all places; it began to give light already through Adam" (*WA* 46, 564, 23–32 [*LW* 22, 33]).

69. *WA* 4, 9, 18.

70. On God-shaped men, see *WA* 56, 388, 31. Cf. Luther's emphasis that the whole of deity lives in the word, *WA* 10^{I,1}, 188, 6–8. Cf. Reinhold Seeberg, *Lehrbuch der Dogmengeschichte*, 2:258; Regin Prenter, *Spiritus Creator*, p. 44. All creation is divine word: "The created word is made through the uncreated word, for what is all creation but the word of God?" (*WA* 42, 17, 29 [*LW* 1, 22]). Men experience daily the same miracle as Israel in passing through the Red Sea: "We live and breathe daily as the children of Israel in the middle of the Red Sea" (*WA* 42, 26, 35 [*LW* 1, 35]). God's creation *ex nihilo* takes place continuously. Maurer (*Von der Freiheit*, p. 86) notes that Luther does not think of this *creatio ex nihilo* in substantialistic categories. *Nihil* means to him "lack of love." Cf. Johannesson, *Person och Gemenskap*, p. 223; A. Siirala, *Gottes Gebot*, pp. 50–103. In speaking about God's action in the word, Luther does not confine the divine efficacy to any one area of reality. "He sends his word and heals them. He is furthermore a God concealed in majesty who neither deplores nor tolerates death but works life, death, and everything in all things. Nor does he merely express himself by his word but retains his freedom over all things" (*WA* 18, 685, 20).

71. Luther on men as means of grace: "Therefore although it takes place through a man's hand, yet it is truly God's own work" *WA* 30^I, 213, 16–17). Cf. *WA* 6, 530, 24–31 (*LW* 36, 62–63). "If you wish to know, see, and reach for God, then see and attend to yourselves. For you are God's work and his work is in you, mutually through you in you" (*WA* 48, 111, 5; cf. *WA* 42, 111, 14 [*LW* 1, 147]).

72. For Luther's criticism of Erasmus's concept of revelation, see *WA* 18, 606, 22–29.

73. On Luther and Aristotle, see Gerrish, *Grace and Reason*, pp. 32–42. On Luther's affirmative relation to Aristotle as a natural scientist, see Lauri Haikola, *Studien zu Luther und zum Luthertum*, pp. 19–24. Luther on Thomas Aquinas and Aristotle: "Thomas has written many heretical things and is the author of the dominance of Aristotle, the devastator of pious doctrine" (*WA* 8, 127, 19).

74. Luther's analysis of the authority of the apostles: "But it happens to imprudent or bad readers of books that they who are weak in the fathers and the saints consider all things to be of the highest authority. It is not the authors but the readers who are to blame. And if one wishes to appeal to the holiness and authority of Saint Peter, he will contend that everything that Saint Peter said at any time is true, so that he is convinced that Peter was speaking the truth even when, according to Matthew 16, weakness of the flesh led him to seek to dissuade Christ from suffering, or when he pleaded with Christ to depart from him and his boat, and many other times when he was rebuked by Christ himself" (*WA* 18, 648, 35; 18, 649, 3).

75. *WA* 18, 616.

76. For Luther's image about the churches of Cain and Abel, see *WA* 42, 220, 40 (*LW* 1, 299); 42, 221, 30 (*LW* 1, 300). "Who knows, if in the total course of the world, from its beginning, the condition of the church of God has not always been such that some are called the people and saints of God who are not actually such, while others among them are truly God's people but are not called such, as the story of Cain and Abel demonstrates?" (*WA* 18, 650, 35).

77. "The kingdom is not being prepared but is already prepared; the sons of the kingdom are being prepared, they do not prepare the kingdom" (*WA* 18, 694, 26). Cf. Haar, *Initium Creaturae Dei*, p. 88.

78. On Luther's charge that the church shatters basic associations of life, see A. Siirala, *Gottes Gebot*, pp. 22–53. Luther speaks of the church of God as a community concealed in his creation. He says that this divine community is imprisoned in the church and in society (*WA* 31^1, 194, 28–32 [*LW* 13, 47]). Ostergaard-Nielsen describes Luther's conception of the basic divine community of life as follows: "When Luther asserts 'that a church is God's creation and order,' he does not intend this to be a dogmatic statement in the sense that only 'reason enlightened by faith' can discover or build such a community. Luther's complaint against the Catholic church is concerned directly with the tyranny with which it enslaves and undermines the personal community of people, which was bestowed already in creation and has therefore always been already present" (*Scriptura Sacra*, p. 34). Cf. Dietrich von Oppen, *The Age of the Person*, pp. 12–21. On *gemeynschaft* and *gemeyne*, see *WA* 6, 293, 1; 31^1, 194, 28 (*LW* 13, 47).

79. *WA* 20, 472, 32. Cf. Kjell Ove Nilsson, *Simul. Das Miteinander von Göttlichem und Menschlichem in Luthers Theologie*, p. 287.

80. *WA* 49, 249, 4.

81. *WA* 26, 294, 23 (*LW* 37, 192).

82. *WA* 40^{II}, 106, 19–25 (*LW* 27, 84–85); 6, 406–7 (*LW* 44, 126–27).

83. *WA* 7, 721, 9.

84. On *Christlich Volk* and *Christenheyt*, see *WA* 6, 300, 37.

85. *WA TR* 2, 248, 38–43. Cf. Nilsson, *Simul*, p. 174. One can confront the divine only by finding men of faith. "Therefore who wants to find Christ must first find the churches. How can one know where Christ and his faith are if he does not know where the believers are? And he who wants to know something about Christ must not trust himself or build his own bridge to heaven but go to the churches. For outside the Christian churches there is no truth, no Christ, no salvation" (*WA* 10^{I,1}, 140, 8–13). Cf. Ostergaard-Nielsen, *Scriptura Sacra*, p. 162.

86. Luther's argument that Christ is not a "private person": "Therefore the whole emphasis is on the particular, 'for you.' We should not present Christ as an innocent and private person (as the Sophists together with all the fathers, Jerome and others, have done), as though he were thus holy and just for himself" (*WA* 40^I, 448, 2–8 [*LW* 26, 287]; cf. *WA* 18, 203, 3 [*LW* 40, 213]; 18, 204, 4 [*LW* 40, 214]). "Out of all this we learn that preaching is inadequate when one preaches Christ's life and work superficially and only as history and chronicle" (*WA* 7, 29, 15).

87. See Kohls, *Theologie des Erasmus*, 1:198.

88. *WA* 43, 672, 40 (*LW* 5, 354).

89. *WA* 18, 738.

90. "I am speaking not about the written but about the spoken gospel, nor about some kind of declamation presented in the churches but about the germane and genuine word" (*WA* 7, 721, 15). Cf. Ostergaard-Nielsen, *Scriptura Sacra*, p. 202.

91. "First of all we are to know that everything that the apostles taught and wrote they drew out of the Old Testament, for in it everything is announced that will take place in the future and be proclaimed in Christ. Therefore they ground all their preaching in the Old Testament, and there is not a word in the New Testament that does not refer back to the Old Testament and is not already announced there" (*WA* 10^{I,1}, 15, 1 [*LW* 35, 122]). Cf. Ostergaard-Nielsen, *Scriptura Sacra*, p. 190.

92. According to Luther, the church is hidden in the field of everyday life, just as the New Testament is hidden in the Old. "We rightly confess in the creed, 'We believe in the holy church.' But it is in an 'inaccessible' place, for its sanctity cannot be seen. God so conceals it and covers it up with infirmities, sins and errors, with various forms of the cross and scandal, that it cannot be reached by our senses" (*WA* 40^{II}, 106, 19 [*LW* 27, 84]).

93. *WA* 40^{I}, 228, 33 (*LW* 26, 129). Cf. Ostergaard-Nielsen, *Scriptura Sacra*, p. 191.

94. *WA* 20, 605, 9 (*LW* 30, 223). Cf. Nilsson, *Simul*, p. 154.

95. To Luther the symbol *word and sacraments* does not express a limited area of reality. "Therefore where baptism, the Lord's Supper, and the divine word are, there men pray, for the church is a house of prayer and Christ has made this house as wide as the whole world" (*WA* 47, 315, 36). Luther stresses that Christ and his church, Christ and his kingdom, are inseparable from each other. Christ is what he is in his church and in his kingdom. "Of the whole Christ, that is, of the kingdom of Christ" (*WA* 18, 210, 35 [*LW* 40, 219]). When Luther speaks of the presence of Christ in the sacraments, he does not speak of a "local" presence but of the way in which Christ is present. He has in mind the sacramental character of life. "How does he see Christ? Must not the eyes be directed high upwards? He is about us and in us in all places. He is everywhere, but he does not want you to grope for him everywhere, but where the word is, there reach for him and you will rightly grasp him. Otherwise you are testing God and end up in idolatry. He has therefore set a definite way for us. If Christ were not with me in prison, torture, and death, where would I be? He is present there along with the word" (*WA* 19, 492, 23 [*LW* 36, 342–43]; 19, 492, 22, 29 [*LW* 36, 342, 343]). "Just as Christ himself and his kingdom are not to be found in any place or in any outward thing, so also everything that belongs to his kingdom is unconfined. . . . So is baptism and also the sacrament. For it is not necessary that one preach, baptize, and receive the sacrament in the church and nowhere else, but rather wherever it is demanded by need. From this it does not follow that Christ in the sacrament is bound to one place, here or there, but with his sacrament he is free to be in all places" (*WA* 18, 211, 19 [*LW* 40, 220]).

96. A typical example of the kind of interpretation of Luther in which he is conceived as presenting a new alternative to the problems of Scholasticism is afforded by R. Seeberg in his history of dogma: "God's general activity is related to his revelation as nature to grace,

law to gospel, reason to faith, the world to the church" (*Lehrbuch der Dogmengeschichte*, 4:162). According to Otto Wolff such an interpretation means that Luther has presented only a variation of the theme of Scholasticism (*Die Haupttypen der neueren Luther-deutung*, p. 309). Cf. Törnvall, *Andligt och världsligt*, pp. 13, 51.

97. Joseph Haroutunian claims that, in its views on the means of grace, contemporary Protestant theology deals with the problems of Scholasticism: "Nevertheless, the traditional dichotomy of those who preach the Word and administer the Sacraments and exercise discipline on the one hand, and those who hear the Word, receive the Sacrament, and undergo discipline is maintained as clearly and sharply as it was in the medieval church. . . . The Reformation doctrine of church—with its insistence upon the external aids necessary for the salvation of the people—perpetuated the Catholic contradistinction between the dispensers and the recipients of grace, and thus, between the clergy and the laity. . . . Roman Catholic institutions and organizations and their priesthood have been replaced by Protestant institutions and organizations and their 'ordained clergy,' and just as Catholics do, Protestants 'go to church' rather than know themselves as the church" (*God with Us: A Theology of Transpersonal Life*, pp. 44–45).

98. On Luther and the "zealots," see A. Siirala, *Gottes Gebot*, 107–20.

99. *WA* 32, 304, 25; 36, 29, 18. Cf. Wingren, *Luther on Vocation*, pp. 162–84. Every man experiences the presence of the divine in his own field of life. In refusing to share in the work of creation man flees from the divine command and promise: "For thus God creates, sustains, serves and rules the children of men . . . and thus underneath human activity faith sees the concealed power of God to perform all things, while the unbelievers erroneously consider only the work of man and ignore the power of God" (*WA* 14, 576, 37 [*LW* 9, 40–41]). "Our action is allowing God to act in us. . . . It is the Lord who performs all our acts in us" (*WA* 2, 539, 5–10 [*LW* 27, 294]). "But he does not work without us; as he recreates and conserves these things in the situation itself, he operates in us and we cooperate with him" (*WA* 18, 754, 10). Cf. Ragnar Bring, *Förhållandet mellan tro och gärningar inom Luthersk teologi*," pp. 11–114; Otto Gühloff, *Gebieten und Schaffen in Luthers Auslegung des ersten Gebotes*, p. 52; Maurer, *Von der Freiheit*, pp. 93–95.

100. On the intertwining of the divine and the human: "What then are human beings, where faith and the word rule, other than some kind of masks of God beneath which he is concealed as he performs

his wonderful works" (*WA* 14, 577, 33 [*LW* 9, 41]). "To serve God is not bound to one or two works or contained in one or two situations, but it encompasses all works and in it all situations share" (*WA* 10[I,1], 413, 8). Cf. Bring, *Förhallandet*, p. 186; Maurer, *Von der Freiheit*, p. 84; Haikola, *Studien zu Luther*, pp. 52–55. The divine has been present as "word and sacraments" from the beginning of the world: "For there are three kinds of regiment on earth. The first is his heavenly kingdom, that is, his divine word and God's service, where he rules over conscience and soul through preaching, baptism, or sacrament. This is the highest and most excellent; thus he directs things from the beginning to the end of the world" (*WA* 37, 426, 7; cf. *WA* 47, 583, 35; 50, 652, 18 [*LW* 41, 177]). The gospel is not itself the light but a witness to the light which has shone from the beginning of the world: "For the New Testament is nothing more than a revelation of the Old" (*WA* 10[I,1], 181, 24); "It is this same spirit which was in each particular age in Job, in Abraham, in Adam" (*WA* 8, 69, 19 [*LW* 32, 176]).

101. On the inseparability of word and faith, see *WA* 6, 514 (*LW* 36, 38–39); 10[I,1], 159, 21; 10[I,1], 160, 2. Cf. Maurer, *Von der Freiheit*, p. 101. See Otto Ritschl's criticism of fideistic interpretations, *Dogmengeschichte des Protestantismus*, 1:80.

102. On Luther's conception of faith as the basic situation of life, see A. Siirala, *Gottes Gebot*, pp. 53–105; Haar, *Initium Creaturae Dei*, p. 20. On the network of faith and love, see George W. Forell, *Faith Active in Love*, pp. 70–112.

103. Luther's view of man as seed sown in the field of life: "Our Lord God is a good plowman who casts us all in his pouch" (*WA* 49, 426, 36; cf. *WA* 37, 70, 5). "By the day of the gospel Paul means a day when we see the dawn, as all birds sing, all animals begin to stir, all men rise up, and it appears as though the whole world were new and alive at the break of day" (*WA* 49, 427, 37). Cf. Haar, *Initium Creaturae Dei*, p. 62. Man has the seed of the future, "he is sown for the summer to come" (*WA* 36, 643, 29). The word of the gospel is life's own word: "From this we see how the same light has gone forth from the beginning of the world again and again and still goes forth. This life and light is always in the world and gives it life" (*WA* 46, 566, 26–31 [*LW* 22, 35]). "I say this in order that we may know how the light of Christ himself has gone forth from the beginning of the world and has done much good in the world with its creative radiance" (*WA* 46, 567, 15–18 [*LW* 22, 36]). "Christ is the head of his church from the beginning to the very end of the world" (*WA* 6, 553, 5 [*LW* 36, 95]; 37, 426, 7 ff.). Cf. Gerhard Ebeling, *God and Word*, p. 27. When Luther

speaks about the omnipresent activity of God, he presents not peripheral speculation but the core of the message of the gospel. Cf. Friedrich Gogarten, *Die Verkündigung Jesu Christi*, p. 334.

104. *WA* 56, 415, 22.

105. *WA* 40^I, 589, 8 [*LW* 26, 387]; 56, 388, 27.

106. On Erasmus's concept of man, see Winter, *Erasmus–Luther*, pp. 48–63. On Erasmus's skepticism, see Kohls, *Theologie des Erasmus*, 1:61. On his relation to Scholasticism, see ibid., 2:86.

107. According to Luther, knowing God and knowing oneself are inseparable. "For as the hearts are fixed, so also history and revelation dispatch themselves. Revelations take place in keeping with the minds in which they occur" (*WA* 23, 511, 7). "My fate accords with the way I think about God" (*WA* 40^{II}, 343 [cf. *LW* 12, 335–36]). "The human heart and the human will are necessary for justification; they must also be present" (*WA* 39^I, 214, 26). "He changes in the manner in which we change, he is in us as our conscience is" (*WA* 14, 448). "But there are sayings which show the nature of faith. These may be called 'God thoughts,' when we feel and inwardly prove that he is doing the thinking. So it all proceeds thus: the position which I assume toward God is also the position which he assumes toward me. In the way in which conscience is altered toward God, so is also the speech of Scripture altered, for it speaks exactly as man feels it as speaking. Therefore all this means nothing else than that God stirs the heart through the external action. As the heart feels, so God may be said to sleep, rise, work, and speak" (*WA* 24, 206, 22; 24, 231, 17; cf. *WA* 18, 754, 24; 18, 769; 18, 778). Cf. Hans-Joachim Iwand, *Rechtfertigungslehre und Christusglaube;* G. K. Ljunggren, *Synd och skuld i Luthers teologi*, pp. 148–87.

108. Jaeger's description of the theology of Plato and Aristotle: "When Plato and Aristotle, following in Socrates' footsteps, re-established the certainty of God as the supreme principle of the natural and social world, they did not mean to return to the mythological age, but they wanted to reveal the indestructible kernel of reality which religion in its mythical stage had symbolized in mythical form. Therefore they now approached that reality which religion called theos by means of reason, or as the Greek language says logos. The result of this intellectual effort is called theologia. The man who coined the word and established the new concept as the center of all philosophical thought was Plato. . . . It was the people of the Greeks, the founders of philosophy and science, who contributed to the intellectual life of mankind this new form of rational approach to the

superhuman world" (*Humanism and Theology*, pp. 45–46). Jaeger notes that it is characteristic of Greek philosophy to speak of the *nature* of man. " 'Nature' is a Greek concept which implies a specific mental approach to reality. Its admission includes the acceptance of a perfectly objective attitude of the observer's mind towards the world. Every theology which takes over this idea thereby admits that the rational approach to reality is of fundamental importance for its task" (ibid., p. 17).

Jaeger's presentation makes clear that the view of man as primarily a disciple of reality is derived from the Greek concept of *paideia*. "As the ancient grammarian Aulus Gellius . . . rightly observes, the Latin humanitas . . . corresponds to the Greek paideia. . . . Cicero ascribes to the Greek spirit a humanizing influence; it helps man to discover his true self and thereby shape his personality. It exercises that influence because it puts before our eyes with overwhelming clarity that ideal pattern of humanity which stirs our admiration and with it one of the most powerful of human instincts, imitation" (ibid., p. 21). Against this background it becomes apparent that Luther's criticism of the *imitatio* piety of his heritage touched the foundations not only of the church but of the whole traditional culture as well. Cf. Georg H. von Wright, *Ajatus ja julistus*, pp. 11–32. Luther stresses that walking in the company of Jesus is not "imitation" but sharing in the new creation: "Truly to put on Christ, in an evangelical way, is not a matter of imitation but of new birth and new creation" (*WA* 40^I, 540, 17 [LW 26, 352]). See Ragnar Bring, *Dualismen hos Luther*, pp. 40–50. The church of God is a coming reality, a new human race (*WA* 4, 444, 28–40).

109. On universals as realities or mere names, see Johannesson, *Person och Gemenskap*. For the interpretation of Luther in the framework of nominalism, see R. Seeberg, *Lehrbuch*, 4:1, 92; Bengt Hägglund, *Theologie und Philosophie bei Luther in der occamistischen Tradition*.

110. Luther argues that as man flees thinking he flees life. God's omnipresent activity is manifest both in Scripture and in experience so clearly that even a child can understand it: "Nor can one use here the pretext of the obscurity of Scripture or the difficulty of the matter. The words are so completely clear that a child can understand them. The matter is so plain and easy that it can be proved by the natural judgment of common sense" (*WA* 18, 719, 1). Luther says that man would rather blame himself and explain everything by the categories of cause and effect than acknowledge the presence of the divine in human life (*WA* 18, 718).

Faith in God as creator is no preliminary stage of faith proper. The first article of the creed is to Luther the most difficult and the highest (*altissimus*). Christ leads Christians to it (*WA* 11, 49, 3). Cf. Törnvall, *Andligt och världsligt*, p. 181.

111. Cf. William F. Lynch's description of the absolutizing instinct as a major factor in the illness and fragmentation of the human mind: "By the absolutizing instinct I mean something very literal and nothing complicated. I mean the instinct in human beings that tends to absolutize everything. . . . The instinct's whole drive is to make absolutes out of everything it touches and to pour floods of fantasy into the world about it. It is the father of all hopeless projects and hopelessness. It is the enemy of the human and of hope. . . . The absolutizing instinct magnifies. In its presence each thing loses its true perspective and its true edges. The good becomes tremendously good, the evil becomes absolutely evil, the grey becomes the black or white, the complicated, because it is difficult to handle, becomes, in desperation, the completely simple. . . . But above all, everything assumes a greater weight than it has, and becomes a greater burden. . . . The absolutizing instinct is the father of the hopeless and adds that special feeling of weight that hopelessness attaches to everything it touches. It is, in general, the creator of hopeless projects and the creator of idols" (*Images of Hope: Imagination as Healer of the Hopeless*, pp. 106–7). Lynch, a Catholic literary critic and theologian, wrote *Images of Hope* in the setting of a hospital for the mentally ill. In his preface he refers to the research by Martti Siirala (*Medicine in Metamorphosis*, pp. 5–6). Here is an encouraging example of the interaction between different areas of the study of man which was discussed in the opening section of the present study. Cf. Martti Siirala, "On Some Relations between Thought and Hope."

112. Luther's evaluation of the Greek orientation to life: "Nor is it proper to label as barbarians those whom the Holy Spirit is willing to use. We should rather call the elegance of the Greeks barbaric insofar as it is coupled with irreligion and ignorance of God" (*WA* 40^{III}, 459, 22).

113. Luther's conception of human existence as growth: "In this life we are his creatures in the stage of beginning" (*WA* 45, 80, 36), "first-fruits of his creation" (*WA* 41, 587, 20). Cf. Haar, *Initium Creaturae Dei*, pp. 84, 95. For images of birth, child, growth, see *WA* 40^{II}, 428; 46, 617, 17 [*LW* 22, 94]; 18, 754; 14, 140, 32. Cf. Aarne Siirala, "Verbum och creatura i Luthers bibelutläggning." On creation as stretching toward the future, see *WA* 42, 87, 6–23 [*LW* 1, 115]; 56, 371. On Christ in us as new humanity: "Thus there are two men in us, Adam and Christ, the one old, the other new" (*WA* 1, 81, 8). Cf. Erich Seeberg, *Luthers Theologie*, 2:86; Haar, *Initium Creaturae Dei*.

114. On Luther's relation to the child and childhood, see Erikson, *Young Man Luther*, pp. 99, 119.

115. See Aldridge, *Hermeneutic of Erasmus*, p. 96.

116. On Plato and Augustine, and on Aristotle and Thomas, see Nygren, *Agape and Eros;* Johannesson, *Person och Gemenskap.* On Plato and medieval theology, see Ernst Hoffman, *Platonismus und Christliche Philosophie.*

117. On law and gospel, and on nature and grace, see A. Siirala, *Gottes Gebot*, pp. 267–352.

118. On the structure of medieval universities, see Ebeling, *Luther,* pp. 29–47.

119. For Jaeger's evaluation of Erasmus, see *Humanism and Theology,* p. 65. For his evaluation of Thomas, see ibid., pp. 30–35.

120. On Erasmus's exegetical principles, see Aldridge, *Hermeneutic of Erasmus*, pp. 96–100.

121. Huizinga, *Erasmus*, p. 161. Cf. Olin, *Desiderius Erasmus*, p. 145. The leadership of the church brought pressure on Erasmus to write against Luther (Huizinga, *Erasmus*, p. 161). Luther tried to express conceptually what cannot be verbalized (ibid., p. 163); cf. Osmo Tiililä, *Systemaattinen teologia*, 2:46; Bring, *Dualismen hos Luther*, p. 153.

122. On "scientism" and "revealed knowledge," see Aarne Siirala, *The Voice of Illness: A Study in Prophecy and Therapy*, pp. 51–64, 124–41.

123. For Luther's statement on suffering, existence, and action, see *WA* 56, 117, 21.

124. On Luther's estimate of Erasmus as a person, see Flitner, *Erasmus,* pp. 12–13.

125. See Winter, *Erasmus-Luther*, pp. 9, 22–24.

126. For Luther's description of man's "fall" into the knowledge of good and evil as "rising," see *WA* 14, 130, 35; 14, 131, 32. Cf. Dietrich Bonhoeffer: "The knowledge of good and evil seems to be the aim of all ethical reflection. The first task of Christian ethics is to invalidate this knowledge. . . . Already in the possibility of the knowledge of good and evil Christian ethics discerns a falling away from the origin. Man at his origin knows only one thing: God. It is only in the unity of his knowledge of God that he knows of other men, of things, and of himself. He knows all things only in God, and God in all things.

The knowledge of good and evil shows that he is no longer at one with this origin. . . . Only against God can man know good and evil. . . . Man knows good and evil, against God, against his origin, godlessly and of his own choice, understanding himself according to his own contrary possibilities; and he is cut off from the unifying, reconciling life in God, and is delivered over to death. . . . Man's life is now disunion with God, with men, with things, and with himself" (*Ethics*, pp. 17–20).

127. According to Luther, Erasmus's main error is his conception of the basic situation of humanness in terms of the knowledge of good and evil. Man is thus understood as being capable of bearing the responsibility for his own life. To Luther this is impossible. Life is based on forgiveness. For this reason a man who barricades himself behind self-accusation and self-defense denies the gospel. An accusing conscience is actually *evil* conscience. "When man bases his life on his own conscience, he is blind to the reality of sin. God's command creates a new conscience and discloses above all what man is not and does not realize, that he does not believe. Through God's command and faith man's guilt becomes revealed as that which he has not lived. The unbeliever denies this guilt and sticks to his effort to possess his life for himself" (A. Siirala, *Gottes Gebot*, p. 286). Cf. Martti Siirala's presentation of the decisive importance of the "unlived life" for man's development ("Schizophrenia: A Human Situation"; "Self-Creating in Therapy"). Cf. Delton Glebe, "Law and Gospel in Pastoral Counseling."

128. According to Luther, the divine word is in action to bring about radical change: "Therefore, to wish to silence these tumults is nothing else than to wish to hinder the word of God and to take it out of the way. For the word of God, wherever it comes, comes to change and to renew the world. . . . And as to myself, if I did not see these tumults, I would say that the word of God is not in the world. But now, when I do see them, I rejoice from my heart and do not fear them, for I am convinced that the kingdom of the pope with all his followers will fall to the ground. For it is especially against this that the word of God, now at work, is directed. I see indeed, my Erasmus, that you complain in many books about these tumults and the loss of peace and concord. And you attempt many means whereby to afford a remedy and, as I am inclined to believe, with a good intention. But this gouty foot laughs at your doctoring hands, for you are trying to put out fire with straw. Cease from complaining, cease from doctoring. This tumult goes on and is carried on from above" (*WA* 18, 626, 38).

129. "And who has given you the power or committed to you the right to bind Christian doctrine to places, persons, times, and causes,

when Christ wishes it to be proclaimed and to reign most freely throughout the world? The word of God is not bound, says Paul, and is Erasmus now to bind it? Nor did God give us the word that it should be had with respect to places, persons, or times. As Christ says, 'Go into all the world,' not go into this place and not into that, as Erasmus says" (*WA* 18, 628, 35). "To bind the word of God and to stand in the way of the life of men" (*WA* 18, 629, 38). Cf. *WA* 18, 655–57.

130. On man's basic situation as a state of war, see *WA* 24, 116, 26. On existence as conflict between flesh and spirit, see *WA* 18, 743–46.

131. On Erasmus's description of man's basic situation as knowledge of good and evil, see Winter, *Erasmus–Luther*, pp. 23–30.

132. On Luther's conception of man as convalescing from illness, see Aarne Siirala, *The Voice of Illness*, pp. 147–57.

133. On Luther's *theologia crucis* ("theology of the cross"), see ibid., pp. 148–55.

134. See Bring, *Dualismen hos Luther*, p. 211.

135. The cross: crusade or exploration? Through the centuries the cross has been a fundamental symbol of a Christendom which confesses Jesus to be the Christ, God's anointed one. In the study of this symbolism attention has been drawn to the fact that in the history of Christendom there has been a strong tendency to make this symbol the basis of ideological crusades. When the empty and bare cross, on which one does not see a crucified man, becomes the central symbol, it is a symptom of the change of Christian faith into an idealistic concept and the transformation of Christian theology into an ideology of the cross.

Luther perceived this ideological, crusadingly imperialistic spirit to be conducive to a fragmentation of man and of the fabric of humanity. His life and thought tell of the enchanting power of a spirit which absolutizes man's ideas and experiences. Both his theology and his activity are replete with striking expressions which manifest the power of this spirit to draw men into its vortex. This influence is evident in a particularly tragic way in his writings against the Jews, which have given rise to horrifying ideological crusading. These elements in his theology, which the present writer has discussed in another connection (see "Luther and the Jews") show the central importance of Luther's insight that man is simultaneously righteous and a sinner (*simul justus et peccator*), at the same time convalescent and ill, rising

from the dead and dead, living by promise and breaking it, abiding by
the covenants of life and violating them, new man and old man. On the
other hand, his thought and life speak powerfully of the presence in
our midst of the divine humanness which he proclaimed in setting
forth the gospel, the good news of the manifestation of life in the
birth, human growth, death, and resurrection of Jesus. The proclamation of this good news, as we have attempted to show, contains an
abundance of material which is opposed to theological crusading and
which leads to an exploration in quest of the treasure hidden in the
field of life, divine humanness. When Luther speaks in New Testament
symbols about the reality of the divine humanness, he says that the
exaltation of the Son of man to the right hand of God signifies the
resurrection of man throughout all creation. At the right hand of the
Father is his creation. What takes place in Jesus takes place for us
and in us. In Jesus the divine humanness which in us is crucified and
dying is resurrected and exalted to be the light of life. *Ecce homo*
does not focus our vision upon an idea or upon an ideal man but
impels us to seek contact in men with the divine humanness which
breaks down inhumanness.

136. "A theologian of the cross (that is, one who speaks of God as
crucified and concealed) teaches that punishments, crosses and death
are the most precious treasure of all" (*WA* 1, 613, 21).

137. For Luther's prayer "Come, Lord Jesus," see *WA* 42, 2, 30. Cf.
Haar, *Initium Creaturae Dei*, p. 114; Iwand, *Rechtfertigungslehre*, p.
54; Wingren, *Luther on Vocation*, pp. 53–55.

3. Openness to What Is to Come

1. On times of crisis and the study of man, see Paul E. Pfuetze, *Self,
Society, Existence*, pp. 19–37; Martin Buber, *I and Thou;* Hans E.
Hengstenberg, *Philosophische Anthropologie*, pp. 1–6.

2. On communistic social pathology, see F. S. C. Northrop, *The Meeting of East and West*, pp. 20–253; Reinhold Niebuhr, *Man's Nature
and His Communities*, pp. 37–39.

3. On the value of pluralistic culture, see Michael Polanyi: "Applied
to human affairs, the Laplacean universal mechanics induces the teaching that material welfare and the establishment of an unlimited power
for imposing the conditions of material welfare are the supreme good.
. . . The comprehensive claims of this movement leave no justification to public liberties, and demand that all cultural activities should
subserve the power of the State in transforming society for the achieve-

ment of welfare. A discovery will then no longer be valued by the satisfaction which it gives to intellectual passions of scientists, but will be assessed according to its probable utility for strengthening public power and improving the standard of living" (*Personal Knowledge*, p. 142). Cf. Niebuhr, *Man's Nature*, p. 27.

4. Ludwig Wittgenstein on the philosopher as one who deals with sickness, see *Philosophical Investigations*, par. 255; on the variety of therapeutic methods, ibid., par. 133; on the image of the fly and the bottle, ibid., par. 369. Cf. Walter Kaufmann, *Critique of Religion and Philosophy*, p. 57.

5. See *Expo 67: Official Guide*. Cf. Herbert Marshall McLuhan: "After three thousand years of explosion, by means of fragmentary and mechanical technologies, the Western world is imploding. During the mechanical ages we had extended our bodies in space. Today, after more than a century of electric technology, we have extended our central nervous system itself in global embrace, abolishing both space and time as our planet is concerned. Rapidly, we approach the final phase of the extensions of man in the technological stimulation of consciousness, when the creative process of knowing will be collectively and corporately extended to the whole human society, much as we have already extended our senses and our nerves by the various media. . . . The aspiration of our time for wholeness, empathy and depth of awareness is a natural adjunct of electric technology. . . . The mark of our time is its revulsion against imposed patterns. We are suddenly eager to have things and people declare their beings totally" (*Understanding Media: The Extensions of Man*, pp. 3, 5).

6. In September 1967 Waterloo Lutheran University held a theological conference dealing with Expo. The material here presented has been taken mainly from the presentation of Dr. Gregory Baum, Catholic theologian. A mimeographed copy of his manuscript is in the university library. Cf. Gregory Baum, "Ecumenism after Vatican Council II," p. 52.

7. On the language crisis within the denominations, see Regin Prenter, *Creation and Redemption*, pp. 1–35.

8. Martti Siirala, *Medicine in Metamorphosis*, pp. 125–26, 91–92.

9. On violence in the relations between the generations, see Konrad Lorenz, *On Aggression*, pp. 220–36; Philip H. Phenix, *Man and His Becoming*, pp. 52–59.

10. See Gotthard Booth, "Irrational Complications of the Cancer Problem."

11. Hengstenberg on the central importance of life's basic associations for human existence: "But modern anthropology is thus involved in a dilemma which may be formulated in this way: in times of social harmony the anthropological question does not arise; when the social relationship is disturbed, it cannot be rightly answered. . . . There remains only one way: to address man at that point and to interpret him from that point where he is still capable of communal relations (in the widest sense)" (*Philosophische Anthropologie*, pp. 3–4). Cf. Fritz Pappenheim's analysis of the concepts *Gemeinschaft* and *Gesellschaft*, in *The Alienation of Modern Man*.

12. For Eugen Rosenstock-Huessy's portrayal of cruciform reality, see *The Christian Future; or, the Modern Mind Outrun*, pp. 167–71.

13. Winston Churchill, *A Roving Commission*, p. 113.

14. For Paul Tillich's presentation of levels and dimensions, see his *Systematic Theology*, 2:12–16. Cf. Aarne Siirala, "Paul J. Tillich," p. 114.

15. On Descartes, see Eugen Rosenstock-Huessy, *Out of Revolution: Selfbiography of Modern Man*, pp. 630–60. Cf. Karl R. Popper, *The Logic of Scientific Discovery;* Paul Ernst Cassirer, *Descartes. Lehre, Persönlichkeit, Wirkung;* Alistair C. Crombie, *Augustine to Galileo.*

16. On Erasmus's autobiography, *Compendium Vitae*, see John C. Olin, *Desiderius Erasmus: Christian Humanism and the Reformation.*

17. Werner Jaeger on the Sophists and Plato, see *Humanism and Theology*, pp. 50–54. Cf. Gerhard Ebeling, *Theologie und Philosophie*, p. 728; Philip Rieff, *The Triumph of the Therapeutic*, p. 68.

18. On Aristotle's view of *polis*, see Niebuhr, *Man's Nature*, pp. 33–35; Rieff, *Triumph of the Therapeutic*, p. 68.

19. Rieff on the idealistic structuring of society, see *Triumph of the Therapeutic*, pp. 66–68; on radical democratic individualism, see ibid., p. 70.

20. See F. S. C. Northrop, *The Meeting of East and West*, pp. 71–91.

21. On Luther and Freud, see Aarne Siirala, *The Voice of Illness: A Study in Prophecy and Therapy*. On Freud as transmitter of the patients' message, see Gustaf Bally, "Sociological Aspects of Psychoanalysis."

22. On research in social pathology, see Gotthard Booth, "Values in Nature and Psychotherapy"; Wilhelm Kütemeyer, *Die Krankheit in*

ihrer Menschlichkeit; Robert A. Lambourne, *Community, Church and Healing;* Martti Siirala, "Our Changing Conception of Illness"; Victor von Weizsäcker, *Soziale Krankheit und soziale Gesundung.* Cf. Aarne Siirala, "Krankheit und Gesundheit in der Menschlichen Gesellschaft."

23. On Comte, see Nygren, *Filosofi och motivforskning,* pp. 168–86.

24. See Barry Boeckner, "The Contributions of a Theological Methodology to an Understanding of Man in the Light of Interdisciplinary Studies."

25. See William B. Kimmel, *Dimensions of Faith.* Cf. Karl Barth, *The Humanity of God.*

26. See Otto A. Piper, "Protestant Theology's Predicament."

27. See Weston La Barre, *The Human Animal.*

28. The following references are to Polanyi, *Personal Knowledge,* pp. 71–82, 87–88 (cf. Ludwig Wittgenstein, *Tractatus Logico-Philosophicus* [London, 1922], p. 1889), 104–17, 142–45, 249–50.

29. See Aarne Siirala, "Implications of the Personalistic Era for Theological Education."

30. Polanyi, *Personal Knowledge,* pp. 49–63.

31. Erik H. Erikson on the breakdown of confidence in the "world of reception" as the most tragic injury to human development: "The failure of basic trust and of mutuality has been recognized in psychiatry as the most far-reaching failure, undercutting all development" (*Insight and Responsibility,* p. 231).

32. See James Barr, "Revelation through History in the Old Testament and Modern Theology."

33. On the Greek concept of language, see Eulalio R. Baltazar, "Teilhard de Chardin: A Philosophy of Procession"; Harald Ostergaard-Nielsen, *Scriptura Sacra et Viva Vox;* Herbert G. Gadamer, "Die Sprache."

34. Aarne Siirala, "Luther and the Jews"; cf. other articles.

35. On the "resistance" of the New Testament to the formulation of the concept of the church, see Ulrich S. Leupold, "The New Testament Concept of *Authority* and Its Bearing on the Meaning of the Ministry."

Bibliography

Aland, Kurt. *Kirchengeschichtliche Entwürfe*. Gütersloh: Mohn, 1960.

Alanen, Yrjö J. E. *Valinta ja Vastuu*. Helsinki: Söderström, 1955.

Aldridge, John W. *The Hermeneutic of Erasmus*. Richmond: Knox, 1966.

Althaus, Paul. *The Divine Command*. Philadelphia: Fortress, 1966.

———. *Luthers Haltung im Bauernkrieg*. Basel: Schwabe, 1953.

Aries, Philippe. *Centuries of Childhood*. New York: Knopf, 1962.

Bainton, Roland H. *Erasmus of Christendom*. New York: Scribner, 1969.

———. *The Reformation of the Sixteenth Century*. Boston: Beacon, 1956.

Bally, Gustaf. "Sociological Aspects of Psychoanalysis." *Bulletin of New York Academy of Medicine* 42 (1966).

Baltazar, Eulalio R. "Teilhard de Chardin: A Philosophy of Procession." In *New Theology*, vol. 2, edited by Martin E. Marty and Dean G. Peerman. New York: Macmillan, 1965.

Barr, James. "Revelation through History in the Old Testament and Modern Theology." In *New Theology*, vol. 1, edited by Martin E. Marty and Dean G. Peerman. New York: Macmillan, 1964.

Barth, Karl. *The Humanity of God*. Richmond: Knox, 1960.

Baum, Gregory. "Ecumenism after Vatican Council II." *Consilium* 10 (1967).

Beintker, Horst. *Die Uberwindung der Anfechtung bei Luther*. Berlin: Evang. Verlagsanstalt, 1954.

Blanke, Fritz. *Der Verborgene Gott bei Luther*. Berlin: Furche, 1928.

Boeckner, Barry. "The Contributions of a Theological Methodology to an Understanding of Man in the Light of Interdisciplinary Studies." Mimeographed. Waterloo, Ont.: Waterloo Lutheran University, 1967.

Bohlin, Torgny. *Den Korsfäste Skaparen*. Stockholm: Diakonistyrelse, 1952.

Boisset, Jean. *Erasme et Luther*. Paris: Presses Universitaires, 1962.

Bonhoeffer, Dietrich. *Ethics*. Edited by Eberhard Bethge. New York: Macmillan, 1955.

———. *The Communion of Saints*. New York: Harper, 1963.

Booth, Gotthard. "Values in Nature and Psychotherapy." *Archives of General Psychiatry* 8 (1963).

————. "Irrational Complications of the Cancer Problem." *The American Journal of Psychoanalysis* 25, no. 1.

Bornkamm, Heinrich. *Luthers geistige Welt*. Lüneburg: Heliand, 1947.

————. *Luther and the Old Testament*. Philadelphia: Fortress, 1969.

————. "Erasmus and Luther." In *Luther-Jahrbuch*. Berlin: Luth. Verlagshaus, 1958.

————. "Faith and Reason in the Thought of Erasmus and Luther." In *Religion and Culture*, edited by W. Leibrecht. New York: Harper, 1959.

Bouyer, Louis. *Erasmus and His Times*. Baltimore: Newman, 1959.

Bring, Ragnar. *Dualismen hos Luther*. Lund: Ohlson, 1929.

————. *Förhållandet mellan tro och gärningar inom Luthersk teologi*. Acta Acadeamiae Aboensis, Humaniora 9. Helsingfors, 1933.

————. "Kring uppgörelsen mellan Erasmus och Luther." In *Till Gustaf Aulén*. Lund, 1939.

————. *Kristendomstolkningar i gammal och i ny tid*. Stockholm, 1950.

Brunner, H. Emil. *Der Mensch im Widerspruch*. Berlin: Furche, 1937.

Buber, Martin. *I and Thou*. New York: Scribner, 1958.

Cassirer, Paul Ernst. *Descartes. Lehre, Persönlichkeit, Wirkung*. Stockholm: Bermann-Fischer, 1939.

————. *An Essay on Man*. New York: Doubleday, 1953.

Churchill, Winston. *A Roving Commission*. New York: Scribner, 1930.

Crombie, Alistair C. *Augustine to Galileo*. London: Heinemann, 1957.

Davies, Rupert E. *The Problem of Authority in the Continental Reformers*. London: Epworth, 1946.

Denifle, Heinrich. *Luther und Luthertum in der ersten Entwicklung*. Mainz: Kirchheim, 1906.

Dolfen, Christian. *Die Stellung des Erasmus von Rotterdam zur scholastischen Methode*. Osnabrück: Meinders, 1936.

Doniger, Simon, ed. *The Nature of Man*. New York: Harper, 1962.

Ebeling, Gerhard. "Theologie und Philosophie." In *Religion in Geschichte und Gegenwart*, vol. 6. Tübingen: Mohr, 1961.

————. *Luther. Einfuhrüng in sein Denken*. Tübingen: Mohr, 1965. (English translation *Luther: An Introduction to His Thought* to be published spring 1970 by Fortress Press.)

————. *God and Word*. Philadelphia: Fortress, 1967.

Elert, Werner. *The Structure of Lutheranism*. Saint Louis: Concordia, 1962.

————. *Der Christliche Glaube*. Berlin: Furche, 1940.

————. *The Christian Ethos*. Philadelphia: Fortress, 1957.

Eliade, Mircea. *Myths, Dreams and Mysteries*. New York: Harper, 1960.

Elliott-Binns, Leonard E. *Erasmus the Reformer*. London: Methuen, 1923.

Erikson, Erik H. *Young Man Luther: A Study in Psychoanalysis and History.* New York: Norton, 1958.

———. *Insight and Responsibility.* New York: Norton, 1964.

Exner, Helmut. *Der Einfluss des Erasmus auf die englische Bildungsidee.* Berlin: Junker, 1939.

Expo 67: Official Guide. Montreal: Maclean-Hunter, 1967.

Flitner, Andreas. *Erasmus in Urteil seiner Nachwelt.* Tübingen: Niemeyer, 1952.

Forell, George W. *Faith Active in Love.* New York: American Press, 1954.

Freud, Sigmund. *Autobiography.* New York: Norton, 1935.

Gadamer, Herbert G. "Die Sprache." In *Religion in Geschichte und Gegenwart,* vol. 7. Tübingen: Mohr, 1962.

Gerrish, Brian A. *Grace and Reason.* New York: Oxford University Press, 1962.

Glebe, Delton. "Law and Gospel in Pastoral Counseling." *Pastoral Psychology,* December 1965.

Gogarten, Friedrich. *Die Verkündigung Jesu Christi.* Heidelberg: Schneider, 1948.

Grisar, Hartmann. *Luther.* 6 vols. London: Kegan, 1913–17.

Gühloff, Otto. *Gebieten und Schaffen in Luthers Auslegung des ersten Gebotes.* Dissertation, University of Göttingen, 1939.

Haar, Johann. *Initium Creaturae Dei.* Gütersloh: Bertelsmann, 1939.

Hägglund, Bengt. *Theologie und Philosophie bei Luther in der occamistischen Tradition.* Lund: Gleerup, 1955.

Haikola, Lauri. *Gesetz und Evangelium bei Matthias Flacius Illyricus.* Lund: Gleerup, 1952.

———. *Studien zu Luther und zum Luthertum.* Uppsala: Lundquist, 1958.

———. *Usus Legis.* Uppsala: Lundquist, 1958.

Harbison, E. Harris. *The Christian Scholar in the Age of Reformation.* New York: Scribner, 1956.

Harmon, John J. "Toward a Theology of the City Church." *Cross Currents* 44 (1964).

Harnack, Theodosius. *Luthers Theologie.* 2 vols. Munich: Kaiser, 1937.

Haroutunian, Joseph. *God with Us: A Theology of Transpersonal Life.* Philadelphia: Westminster, 1965.

Heick, Otto W. *History of Christian Thought.* 2 vols. Philadelphia: Fortress, 1965–66.

Hengstenberg, Hans E. *Philosophische Anthropologie.* Stuttgart: Kohlhammer, 1966.

Hermann, Rudolf. *Luthers These "Gerecht und Sünder zugleich."* Gütersloh: Mohn, 1930.

Hoffmann, G. "Luthers Streit mit Erasmus." *Zeitschrift für systematische Theologie* 8 (1936).

Hoffman, Ernst. *Platonismus und Christliche Philosophie.* Stuttgart: Artemis, 1960.

Holl, Karl. *Luther.* Gesammelte Aufsätze zur Kirchengeschichte, vol. 1. Tübingen: Mohr, 1948.

Huizinga, Johann. *Erasmus and the Age of Reformation.* New York: Harper, 1957.

Iwand, Hans-Joachim. *Rechtfertigungslehre und Christusglaube.* Leipzig: Hinrichs, 1930.

Jaeger, Werner. *Paideia: The Ideals of Greek Culture.* 3 vols. New York: Oxford University Press, 1939–44.

———. *Humanism and Theology.* Milwaukee: Marquette, 1943.

Johannesson, Rudolf. *Person och Gemenskap.* Stockholm: Diakonistyrelse, 1947.

Kantonen, T. A. *Risti ja Tähtilippu.* Helsinki: Söderström, 1950.

Kaufmann, Walter. *Critique of Religion and Philosophy.* New York: Harper, 1958.

Kelman, Harold. "Communing and Relating." *American Journal of Psychoanalysis* (1960).

Kimmel, William B. *Dimensions of Faith.* New York: Twayne, 1960.

Kohls, Ernst Wilhelm. *Die Theologie des Erasmus.* 2 vols. Basel: Reinhardt, 1966.

Koskenniemi, A. E., ed. *Martti Luther. Kirkkopostilla III.* Helsinki: Luterilainen Evankeliumi Yhdistys, 1944.

Kütemeyer, Wilhelm. *Die Krankheit in ihrer Menschlichkeit.* Göttingen: Vandenhoeck, 1963.

La Barre, Weston. *The Human Animal.* University of Chicago Press, 1954.

Lambourne, Robert A. *Community, Church and Healing.* London: Barton, 1963.

Lammers, Heinrich. *Luthers Anschauung von Willen.* Berlin: Junker, 1935.

Langer, Susanne K. *Philosophy in a New Key.* New York: New American Library, 1958.

Lecler, Joseph. *Toleration and the Reformation.* New York: Association Press, 1960.

Leupold, Ulrich S. "The New Testament Concept of *Authority* and Its Bearing on the Meaning of the Ministry." Manuscript. Toronto: Faith and Order Study Group of the Canadian Council of Churches, 1966.

Lindström, Valter. "Människan är vad hon tror." In *Talenta quinque.* Helsinki: Söderström, 1953.

Link, Wilhelm. *Das Ringen Luthers um die Freiheit der Theologie von der Philosophie*. Munich: Kaiser, 1955.

Ljunggren, G. K. *Synd och skuld i Luthers teologi*. Stockholm, 1928.

Löfgren, David. *Die Theologie der Schöpfung bei Luther*. Göttingen: Vandenhoeck, 1960.

Lohse, Bernhard. *Ratio und Fides*. Göttingen: Vandenhoeck, 1958.

Lorenz, Konrad. *On Aggression*. New York: Harcourt, 1966.

Lunn, Sir Arthur. *The Revolt against Reason*. London: Eyre, 1950.

Lynch, William F. *Images of Hope: Imagination as Healer of the Hopeless*. Montreal: Helicon, 1965.

McLuhan, Herbert Marshall. *Understanding Media: The Extensions of Man*. New York: McGraw, 1964.

McSorley, Harry J. *Luther: Right or Wrong?* New York: Newman; Minneapolis: Augsburg, 1969.

Manuel, Frank E. *Shapes of Philosophical History*. Palo Alto, Calif.: Stanford University Press, 1964.

Maritain, Jacques. *Three Reformers: Luther, Descartes, Rousseau*. New York: Scribner, 1932.

Marty, Martin E., and Peerman, Dean G., eds. *New Theology*. 4 vols. New York: Macmillan, 1964–67.

Maurer, Wilhelm. *Von der Freiheit eines Christenmenschen*. Göttingen: Vandenhoeck, 1949.

Meissinger, Karl A. *Erasmus von Rotterdam*. Berlin: Nauck, 1948.

Mowrer, Orval Hobart. *The Crisis in Psychiatry and Religion*. Princeton: Van Nostrand, 1961.

———. *The New Group Therapy*. Princeton: Van Nostrand, 1964.

Murray, Robert H. *Erasmus and Luther: Their Attitude to Toleration*. London: S.P.C.K., 1920.

Nicholls, William, ed. *Conflicting Images of Man*. New York: Seabury, 1966.

Niebuhr, Reinhold. *Man's Nature and His Communities*. New York: Scribner, 1965.

Nilsson, Kjell Ove. *Simul. Das Miteinander von Göttlichem und Menschlichem in Luthers Theologie*. Göttingen: Vandenhoeck, 1966.

Northrop, F. S. C. *The Logic of the Sciences and the Humanities*. New York: Macmillan, 1960.

———. *The Meeting of East and West*. New York: Macmillan, 1960.

Nygren, Anders. *Filosofi och motivforskning*. Stockholm, 1940.

———. *Agape and Eros*. Philadelphia: Westminster, 1953.

Olimart, K. E. *Der Begriff der Schöpfungsordnung in der Evangelischen Theologie der Gegenwart*. Essen, 1933.

Olin, John C. *Desiderius Erasmus: Christian Humanism and the Reformation*. New York: Harper, 1965.

Ostergaard-Nielsen, Harald. *Scriptura Sacra et Viva Vox*. Munich: Kaiser, 1957.

Packer, J. I., and Johnston, O. R., eds. *Martin Luther on the Bondage of the Will*. London: James Clarke, 1957.

Pannenberg, Wolfhart. *Was ist der Mensch?* Göttingen: Vandenhoeck, 1964. (English translation *What Is Man?* to be published spring 1970 by Fortress Press.)

Pappenheim, Fritz. *The Alienation of Modern Man*. New York: Monthly Review, 1959.

Pelikan, Jaroslav. *Obedient Rebels*. New York: Harper, 1964.

Percy, Stafford, and Allen, H. M., eds. *Opus epistolarum Erasmi*. Oxford: Clarendon, 1906–47.

Persson, Per Erik. *Sacra Doctrina*. Philadelphia: Fortress, 1969.

Pfuetze, Paul E. *Self, Society, Existence*. New York: Harper, 1961.

Pfurtner, Stephanus. *Luther and Aquinas on Salvation*. New York: Sheed, 1965.

Phenix, Philip H. *Man and His Becoming*. New Brunswick, N. J.: Rutgers University Press, 1964.

Pinomaa, Lennart. *Lutherin kilvoitteleva usko*. Helsinki: Söderström, 1952.

———. *Faith Victorious: An Introduction to Luther's Theology*. Philadelphia: Fortress, 1963.

———, ed. *Teologia etsii suuntaa*. Helsinki: Söderström, 1965.

Piper, Otto A. "Protestant Theology's Predicament." *Theology Today* 20, no. 4 (1964).

Pöhl, Ivar H. *Das Problem des Naturrechtes bei Emil Brunner*. Zurich: Zwingli, 1963.

Polanyi, Michael. *Personal Knowledge*. University of Chicago Press, 1958.

———. *The Study of Man*. University of Chicago Press, 1962.

Popper, Karl R. *The Logic of Scientific Discovery*. New York: Bask Books, 1959.

Prenter, Regin. *Spiritus Creator*. Philadelphia: Fortress, 1953.

———. *Creation and Redemption*. Philadelphia: Fortress, 1967.

Rieff, Philip. *The Triumph of the Therapeutic*. New York: Harper, 1966.

Ritschl, Otto. *Dogmengeschichte des Protestantismus*. 4 vols. Leipzig, 1908–12; Göttingen: Hinrichs, 1926–27.

Ritter, Gerhard. *Erasmus und der deutsche Humanistenkreis*. Freiburg: Wagner, 1937.

Rosenstock-Huessy, Eugen. *The Christian Future; or, the Modern Mind Outrun*. New York: Scribner, 1946.

———. *Out of Revolution: Selfbiography of Modern Man*. New York: Four Wells, 1964.

Rupp, Gordon. *The Righteousness of God: Luther Studies.* London: Hodder, 1953.

Russell, Bertrand. *A History of Western Philosophy.* New York: Simon & Schuster, 1959.

Salakka, Yrjö. *Person und Offenbarung in der Theologie Emil Brunners.* Helsinki: Luther-Agricola Seura, 1960.

Schweingruber, Eduard. *Luthers Erlebnis des unfreien Willen.* Zurich: Gotthelf, 1947.

Seeberg, Erich. *Luthers Theologie.* 2 vols. Stuttgart: Kohlhammer, 1937.

Seeberg, Reinhold. *Lehrbuch der Dogmengeschichte.* 4 vols. Leipzig: Deichert, 1913–20.

Seils, Martin. *Der Gedanke von Zusammenwirken Gottes und des Menschen in Luthers Theologie.* Gütersloh: Mohn, 1962.

Siirala, Aarne. "Lundilaisen teologian käsitys systemaattisen teologian tehtävästä." Manuscript. University of Helsinki Library, 1943.

————. "Verbum och creatura i Luthers bibelutläggning." Mimeographed. University of Lund Library, 1950.

————. "Mitä on spiritualismi?" *Teologinen Aikakauskirja* 6 (1950).

————. *Gottes Gebot bei Martin Luther.* Stuttgart: Evang. Verlagswerk, 1956.

————. "The Meaning of Illness." *Journal of Religion and Mental Health* 1, no. 2 (1962).

————. "Korrelaation metodi Paul Tillichin teologiassa." *Teologinen Aikakauskirja* 1 (1963).

————. *The Voice of Illness: A Study in Prophecy and Therapy.* Philadelphia: Fortress, 1964.

————. "Luther and the Jews." *Lutheran World* 3 (1964).

————. "Paul J. Tillich." In *Teologia etsii suuntaa,* edited by Lennart Pinomaa. Helsinki: Söderström, 1965.

————. "Implications of the Personalistic Era for Theological Education." In *Ambulatio Fidei.* Waterloo, Ont.: Waterloo Lutheran University, 1965.

————. "Krankheit und Gesundheit in der Menschlichen Gesellschaft." In *Okumenische Diskussion.* Geneva, 1966.

Siirala, Aarne, and Siirala, Martti. *Elämän ykseys.* Helsinki: Söderström, 1960.

Siirala, Aarne, and Wagner, Norman. "Aims and Practices of Theological Education." Mimeographed. Waterloo, Ont.: Waterloo Lutheran University Library, 1965.

Siirala, Martti. *Die Schizophrenie des Einzelnen und der Allgemeinheit.* Göttingen: Vandenhoeck, 1961.

————. "Schizophrenia: A Human Situation." *American Journal of Psychoanalysis* 23, 1 (1963).

———. "Self-Creating in Therapy." *American Journal of Psycho-analysis* 23, 2 (1963).

———. "On Some Relations between Thought and Hope." *Acta Philosophica Fennica Fasc.* 18 (1965).

———. "Our Changing Conception of Illness." *Journal of Religion and Health* 5, 2 (1966).

———. *Medicine in Metamorphosis: Speech, Presence, and Integration.* London: Tavistock, 1969.

Skydsgaard, Kristen E. *Metafysik og tro.* Copenhagen, 1937.

Smith, Preserved. *Erasmus: A Study of His Life, Ideals and Place in History.* 1923. New York: Ungar, 1962.

Teilhard de Chardin, Pierre. *The Phenomenon of Man.* New York: Harper, 1959.

Tiililä, Osmo. *Systemaattinen teologia.* 2 vols. Helsinki: Söderström, 1951–54.

Tillich, Paul. *Systematic Theology.* 3 vols. University of Chicago Press, 1951–63.

———. *The Future of Religions.* New York: Harper, 1966.

Todd, John M. *Martin Luther.* London: Burns, 1964.

Törnvall, Gustav. *Andligt och världsligt regemente hos Luther.* Stockholm: Diakonistyrelse, 1940.

Trillhaas, Wolfgang. *Dogmatik.* Berlin: Töpelmann, 1967.

Van Peursen, Cornelius A. *Leib-Seele-Geist.* Gütersloh: Mohn, 1959.

Von Loewenich, Walther. *Theologia crucis.* Munich: Kaiser, 1933.

Von Oppen, Dietrich. *The Age of the Person.* Philadelphia: Fortress, 1969.

Von Weizsäcker, Carl F. *The Relevance of Science: Creation and Cosmogony.* New York: Harper, 1964.

Von Weizsäcker, Victor. *Soziale Krankheit und soziale Gesundung.* Göttingen: Vandenhoeck, 1955.

Von Wright, Georg H. *Ajatus ja julistus.* Helsinki: Söderström, 1966.

Whitehead, Alfred North. *Science and the Modern World.* New York: Macmillan, 1960.

Whorf, Benjamin L. *Language, Thought and Reality.* New York: M.I.T. Press, 1956.

Whyte, Lancelot L. *The Next Development in Man.* New York: New American Library, Mentor Books, 1961.

———. *The Unconscious before Freud.* New York: Doubleday, 1960.

Wingren, Gustaf. *Luther on Vocation.* Philadelphia: Fortress, 1957.

———. *The Living Word.* Philadelphia: Fortress, 1960.

———. *Creation and Law.* Philadelphia: Fortress, 1961.

Winter, Ernst F., trans. and ed. *Erasmus–Luther: Discourse on Free Will.* New York: Ungar, 1961.

Wittgenstein, Ludwig. *Philosophical Investigations.* Oxford: Blackwell, 1963.

Wolff, Otto. *Die Haupttypen der neueren Lutherdeutung.* Stuttgart: Kohlhammer, 1938.

Wünsch, Georg. *Luther und die Gegenwart.* Stuttgart: Evang. Verlagswerk, 1961.

Zeeden, Ernst W. *Martin Luther und die Reformation im Urteil des deutschen Luthertums.* Freiburg: Herder, 1950.

Zickendraht, Karl. *Der Streit zwischen Erasmus und Luther über die Willensfreiheit.* Leipzig: Hinrichs, 1909.

Zweig, Stefan. *Erasmus of Rotterdam.* New York: Viking, 1956.

Index

Type, 10 on 13 and 9 on 11 Janson
Display, Janson

The scientific method has often been regarded by Christians as irrelevant to the theological task. But Aarne Siirala contends that the same spirit of exploration that sends man into the unknown worlds of space and microbiology inspires him to seek divine truth. In *Divine Humanness* Dr. Siirala proposes a contemporary empirical theology based on this spirit of exploration.

Both scientists and theologians tend to become isolated in their own fields, says the author. The interplay of human and divine, however, is best understood through open dialogue between the two methods. Dr. Siirala vitalizes theology by introducing the